Free Falling and other student essays

THIRD EDITION

EDITED BY

PAUL SLADKY

AUGUSTA COLLEGE

ST. MARTIN'S PRESS
NEW YORK

Sponsoring editors: Donna Erickson, Jimmy Fleming
Development editor: Susan Cottenden
Managing editor: Patricia Mansfield Phelan
Project editor: Harold Chester
Production supervisor: Joe Ford
Art director: Lucy Krikorian

Library of Congress Catalog Card Number: 96-67027

Manufactured in the United States of America.

1 0 9 8 7
f e d c b a

For information, write:
St. Martin's Press, Inc.
175 Fifth Avenue
New York, NY 10010

ISBN: 0-312-14903-4

PREFACE

.

As you read this book, I expect that you may be surprised in many ways. I certainly have been, not at the fact that student writers can write so well, but that they ask so much of themselves *as writers*. I am amazed by how these essays push beyond the regions of the easy and the obvious, how they so clearly exceed the formulaic. We have been publishing student writers at Augusta College for several years now, yet I still find myself renewed each time a student discovers how powerful the act of writing is. "Real" writers know: if you give yourself up to it, writing will lead you to wholly unexpected and quite amazing places. Our literary tradition—which these essays now declare themselves a part of— has always sought to thrust readers into hitherto-before-unnoticed aspects of our world. Let me call it the *region of surprise* where writers dwell, where readers hope to tread, and, I believe, where the essays in this volume transport us.

I've taken great pleasure in reading and rereading the two hundred or so essays submitted by student writers from campuses around the country. One of the purposes of *Free Falling* is to celebrate good student writing, not just because it's *student writing*, but because it's *good writing*. The question "what constitutes *good* writing?" is, of course, legitimately and eternally arguable. As you read these essays, I invite you to ponder it. You will undoubtedly find the presence and absence of evidence to support your own conclusion. You will favor certain essays and even love a few, as I certainly do. I invite you, however, to challenge them all. In fact, I encourage you to challenge each one specifically by putting your own work up against it and finding a way to say, "Hey, mine can be as good as that." From there, it is simply a matter

v

of following through and writing yours so it is as good as that, or better, as the student writers selected for this volume have taken it upon themselves to do. The thirty-four essays published here certainly aren't the last word on these topics. They seem more like the first words, in fact, the precursors of the *most important* words, those yet to be written, those that *you* are going to speak and write.

In its essence, *Free Falling* has three primary purposes: *to celebrate* student writing, *to provoke discussion* about what makes writing good, and *to inspire* your own writing by motivating you to jump the nest and see where, as a writer, you might land. Whatever else it accomplishes, the book dramatically raises the curtain for this packed house to gaze upon the power and the glory of student writers finding their way into the region of surprise. That, in my opinion, is an accomplishment well worth celebrating. I hope it contributes a spark to the fires of your imagination.

There are many people I would like to thank, but, first and foremost, I thank the student writers who occupy the desks and labor in the vineyards of first-year English, seeking transformations in this world that begin in what is oftentimes the most difficult place, the transformations within oneself. I also sincerely thank the composition teachers who stand behind those students and who labor with equal commitment to those transformations. Many thanks go to the instructors whose students' work was selected from the hundreds of submissions for inclusion in this third edition: Karla Brown, Hawkeye Community College; Nancy Ethridge, Boise State University; Arthur Henne, Pennsylvania State University, York Campus; Kathleen Jernquist, Brown University; Anthony Kellman, Augusta College; Oswald Mayers, College of Saint Benedict; Marsh Rutter, Southwestern College; and Nancy Sutherland, Augusta College.

My thanks go to the following instructors for their insightful reviews of the second edition: Rita Bova, Columbus State Community College; JoAnn Buck, Guilford Technical Community College; Grace Bailey Burneko, Augusta College; Daniel Clark, Northern Kentucky University; Susan Faulkner, Cedar Valley College; Keith Groff, Holy Family College; Mitzi Harris, Western Wyoming Community College; Ronald J. Heckelman, University of Houston—Downtown; William Hofelt, Juniata College; Michael Hricik, Westmoreland County Community College; Bridget Kilgore-Prugh, Pennsylvania State University, York Campus; Catharine B. Kloss, University of Pittsburgh at Johnstown; Barbara E. L'Eplattenier, Purdue University; Perry Lueders, Southwest State University; Karen Madigan, Western Wyoming Community College; Jennifer Miroglotta, John Carroll University; Suzanne Moore, St. Clair Community College; Sheryl Mylan, Stephen F. Austin State University; Karen Oberg, Kansas City Community College; Virginia Skinner-Linnenberg, North Central Michigan College; Stewart Todd, Auburn University; Nancy Vorkink, Community College of Denver; James Werchan, Ohio State University; and Xuewei Wu, Lakewood Community College.

My thanks to everyone involved with *Choice Voice* at Augusta College, both students who submitted work and teachers who encouraged it, as well as Charles Cooper, Rise Axelrod, Lillie Butler-Johnson, Grace Bailey Burneko, Peggy Cheney, and Karin Sisk, all for invaluable support. And finally, a most special debt of gratitude belongs to Nancy Sutherland and Susan Cottenden, who each offered a terrific haven for ideas and are especially blessed with a sensitivity to student writers and their writing.

Paul Sladky

CONTENTS

.

Contents

Contents

Contents

CHAPTER 1

WHY WE NEED TO PUBLISH STUDENT WRITERS

TO STUDENTS

How should we read a book of essays written by students in composition courses? Does the fact that the writers are students like yourself change the way we read, or ought to read, the essays? Is their work any different from the published "professional" work we normally find in anthologies like this?

Judging from the essays in this volume, I think it's safe to say that the writers here take their purposes every bit as seriously as the pros. I'm struck again and again by how committed and energetic their writing is. Not the least bit sheepish, they are out to seize their readers and provoke response. The tone is not, "Gee, would you *like to* read my work?" and the feel isn't that of "ritual texts" being written for a class assignment and an audience of one. Rather, these are words that clearly belong to writers who believe in what they say, writers who are writing for an audience they know is real.

But the question still remains: How should we read the book?

My students would say, "You should read it with a pencil in your hand, and your ears tuned to the voice speaking on the page." Repeatedly, they tell me how much they learn from reading work published by their peers. Student essays excite them. Such essays suggest possibilities and quietly invite them as student writers to take new perspectives on their own writing, to consider ideas they otherwise wouldn't have considered.

Perhaps the best strategy, then, is simply to read this book as a writer would, absorbing the meaning of each essay and, at the same time, using it to clarify your own ideas and purposes. Study the essays to stim-

1

ulate your writerly inventions and expand your sense of style and form. Let the essays launch you in new directions, inspiring you with things to write about and ways to write about them. Let them validate ideas you've considered but, for one reason or another, have never written about. Get excited when you find yourself thinking, "Shoot. If a peer of mine can write this thing of hers like *that*, then I can sure enough write that thing of mine like *this.*"

I could go on justifying ways to read the essays here. But it would sound too much like a directive that contradicts the essential spirit of the book. The way to read the essays is simply to read them, for no ulterior reason at all. Just read and see what happens. Discover what you enjoy, love, disagree with, even dislike about the style and substance of individual essays. You will find favorites, for sure, and you won't love every single piece, as no reader ever does. Nevertheless, I hope you are enriched for having experienced this student writing and its implicit celebration of authenticity and voice.

At Augusta College, we publish the work of English 101 students in *Choice Voice* magazine, a quarterly publication of the composition program. When students' work appears in *Choice Voice*, the effect on them as writers is quite remarkable. Self-concepts change; confidence grows; motivation inspires; and the quality of written products markedly improves. Somehow, writing for a real audience has that effect.

This, then, raises the most important question: What about *your* writing? Have you thought about publishing it? About letting someone other than your teacher read your work? I don't mean have you fantasized *being* Toni Morrison or Ernest Hemingway. Rather, have you ever worked hard on a piece of writing and thought it turned out to be pretty good, even *really* good, and wondered if others would be moved by it, like you have been, to think or feel more deeply?

If you haven't, let me extend an invitation. Since I want to encourage you to think about writing for publication, I invite you to send your writing to St. Martin's Press to be considered for the next edition of *Free Falling*. You'll find a submission form in the back of this book to send along with your essay. You might, in fact, make this your goal. Trust me, writing for publication helps establish a much clearer focus, purpose, and sense of audience. You begin to think: What would readers of *Free Falling* want or need to know?

Remember that the essays you're about to read started out exactly that way—in a composition class as *very* rough drafts. Also remember that a writer's destiny is never sealed. Ernest Hemingway, before he became "Ernest Hemingway," was a student who needed to write to learn to write. There is no other way. Writers and thinkers are *made* by "applying the seat of the pants to the seat of the chair," as the saying goes. So, let me invite you to pull up a chair. And don't be afraid to send us what you've got.

A RATIONALE AND PRAGMATICS FOR INSTRUCTORS

The Rationale

The question implied in the title of this chapter, "Why We Need to Publish Student Writers," is answered by the experiences of the many instructors whose students' work is included in this anthology: Publication contributes to any model of composition because it supplements and extends, rather than displaces, curricular objectives, whatever those objectives might be. Publication is a proposal for what to *do* with texts once they're written. Thus, the pedagogical options for getting those texts written are not at issue.

In the classroom, the *effects* of writing for publication are quite specific. Writing for publication establishes a genuine purpose for student writers by establishing a genuine audience to write for. Consequently, the outcomes are tangible: publication motivates students to write, creates a strong sense of self-validation for students as writers, and contributes importantly to the improved quality of their written texts. This introductory chapter outlines what I perceive to be the variables in writing for publication that contribute most significantly to these outcomes.

Audience is probably the place to start, since recent composition theory begins with the assumption that writing is a negotiable form of social action. Ruth Mitchell and Mary Taylor, for instance, propose an audience-response model of writing that postulates that "all writing is directed towards an audience and is to be regarded as the written medium of transaction" (250). Following this definition, the success of a text is measured essentially by its *effect on* readers rather than by conformity to formal standards, a position with a theoretical taproot that touches Aristotle.

Yet, in spite of such theoretical arguments for rhetorically situated models of composing, we can only measure their practical success by asking the following questions: Where are the readers postulated by these models? Where is the audience whose response is so crucial?

Who, in effect, are our students writing for? The answers to these questions, unfortunately, come up a bit thin. Although the idea that writers engage in negotiated transaction with readers is theoretically, and even practically, alive in the universe of discourse *outside* the composition classroom, *inside* it, our students know in their bones that genuine, negotiated transaction with readers is, for the most part, purely fiction.

One of the most stubborn problems for classroom teachers remains that of authenticating audience. Short of asking students to write letters to congressional representatives or local newspaper editors, the question persists: How do we create for our students genuine audiences situated in genuine rhetorical situations?

The study that James Britton and his colleagues published in 1975 reveals that student writers, in general, write for an uncomfortably narrow range of functions and audiences in the school setting. In the schools he analyzed, Britton's data showed that 48 percent of the time the relationship between writer and audience was "pupil to examiner"; 39 percent of the time it was "learner to teacher"; and 1.8 percent of the time it was "writer to readers" (130). Only *1.8 percent* of the time were students writing to communicate in genuinely negotiable ways with an unknown audience. Since it isn't difficult to generalize these figures to our college classrooms, neither should it be surprising that Britton's call in 1975 was to expand the audience our student writers write for. Perhaps more disappointing is the fact that twenty years have passed and students frequently still do what Britton calls a "dummy run," producing writing in school settings for a narrow and purely instructional purpose and limited audience.

My purpose here is to suggest that writing for publication is an effective way to establish discourse contexts that move the concept of audience from theory to praxis by creating *genuine audiences* for student writers. At Augusta College, one of the most notable aspects of our writing-for-publication program in first-year English has been the extremely positive response from students. They are continually surprised at the writing they produce and the composing processes they engage to produce it. One writer said to me, "I never thought revising something seventeen times was possible until I wanted to get it published," a comment that might be interpreted to mean that only when this student felt he was getting something *from* the exchange was he willing to contribute something *to* the process.

We might also link this student's comment to the rationale for publishing student writers. It clearly reflects a *motivation*—would a writer write seventeen drafts without being motivated?—as well as the writer's sense of *validation*. You can easily imagine a professional writer making such a statement, but can you imagine a student who, more typically, might think three drafts is cruel and unusual punishment? I think not. A student talking about *seventeen* drafts signifies the unacknowledged shift in status from pupil to writer. The remaining outcome—the improved quality of the texts produced—isn't directly recoverable from this student's utterance, but the inference is fairly substantiated; after seventeen drafts, the writing is *bound to* get better.

Writing for publication helps students accommodate written text to audiences, learn that writing must affect a reader, gain information about how readers respond, and understand how writing is evaluated. In our writing-for-publication program at Augusta College, we've observed that published student discourse reflects increasingly solid academic competence. Our students write and publish thoughtful, serious essays in forms accepted by the broader academic discourse community, the one they seek to join. In this regard, publication appears to remain a function of the classroom discourse that subsumes it. In other words, if the published writing is any indication, students *do* learn something of what we teach, and, given the opportunity to enter a genuinely social discourse, they also learn a great deal more.

Writing for publication creates a model that incorporates both social purposes and textual purposes, what have come to be the more or less competing pedagogical models today. If we examine their battle cries, we could say that "make it real" articulates a social purpose while "make it good (or flawless)" articulates a textual purpose. What's interesting is that writing for publication supports *both* social and textual purposes and simplifies the model by synthesizing the two without compromising either one. If an instructor's approach focuses on the social and contextual dimensions of writing, then writing for publication creates a smooth transition to the textual dimension. Likewise, if the approach focuses on the textual dimension of writing, then writing for publication introduces the social context in a tangibly authentic way that recent research has increasingly directed our attention to. In the process-oriented publishing classroom, neither text nor context is neglected. Once students establish authentic communicative purposes, then revising, polishing, and eliminating surface glitches become natural and motivated concerns. The rationale behind writing for publication is ultimately grounded in the effect that publication has on the writers themselves, what we might summarize as effects of motivation, validation, and textual quality.

The Pragmatics

We might start talking about the pragmatic aspects of publishing student writers by first defining what it means to publish. Rather than considering publication strictly in its formal dimensions — formatting end-product texts to disseminate to an anonymous audience — we might approach a definition from a more basic consideration of publication in its social or *contextual* dimensions, that is, in terms of the relations that hold between readers and texts, and between writers and texts.

From a reader's perspective, the most prominent feature of published text is its status as finished or completed text; a published text is a text the reader, if not the writer, deems no longer "in process." We read published texts by and large for meaning, approaching them first and foremost (albeit unconsciously) as meaningful objects from which we will derive some kind of information or understanding. We read to *experience* the text — listen to its voice, enter its textual space, respond to its meaning. Given this crucial distinction between reading to understand and reading to correct, we might consider as a form of publication any arrangement that enables readers publicly or privately to experience a text rather than seek to improve or "correct" it.

Thus, our definition: *publication* is any public display of completed text that is no longer deemed *in process*. Who does this "deeming" is, of course, another important question that has a fully historical dimension, as anyone who has ever received a rejection letter from an editor can attest. The deeming process that declares a piece of writing worthy and complete is actually quite complex and, although it falls within the domain of relations between writers and texts, much of it lies beyond my purpose here.

Since conditions in the classroom differ, thankfully, from those faced by writers in the publishing industry, the "deeming" process I'm referring to is considerably broader than simple acceptance or rejection of a manuscript. In the classroom, the deeming process can be shared by writer and editor, whoever plays the latter role. I say *whoever* since it needn't necessarily be the instructor, or should I say, entirely the instructor. Responses by peer readers as well as by the instructor can contribute to texts in process and to a writer's decision and final declaration that a piece has achieved its purpose and is now "finished."

From my own perspective, one of the deeper problems in writing instruction today involves the extent to which we force students to bring writing projects to premature closure. Although the time constraints we must work with are quite legitimate from a management standpoint, their effect is arbitrarily to constrain writers in ways that not only deaden their sense of ownership but also the very processes through which they nurture and develop ideas. The use of writing portfolios is one solution that dovetails nicely with writing for publication.

Aside from the consideration of the relations among readers, writers, and texts, the pragmatic question, in a nutshell, is this: How can we transmit our students' finished products to readers other than the instructor and/or their collaborative peer group? Imagination is the only thing that limits our answers. Some of the possibilities are well known and effective, even in a classroom filled with college students, including: reading student work aloud in class; creating classroom anthologies through desktop publishing; establishing departmental magazines that publish student essays on a quarterly or semester basis; and, one of the most exciting, developing an address or datafile on the campus computer network where student work can be published electronically.

Concerning electronic publishing, the possibilities for exceeding the limitations of print are, of course, endless. At Augusta College, we simply established an academic datafile on the campus network, called it *Choice Voice*, and filled it with past and present issues of our *Choice Voice* magazine. More far-reaching avenues include establishing a home page on the World Wide Web or developing thematically focused web sites where students can contribute discourse on particular questions or issues. As you can imagine, the Internet provides a highly authentic and expanding audience in a rhetorically rich field, all of which is waiting to be developed and explored by composition teachers and their students.

To give you a clearer sense of how writing for publication can be approached in first-year composition courses, it might perhaps be useful to offer a case history of our experience with writing for publication at Augusta College. It certainly isn't a new idea to create a campus-based publication that is devoted exclusively to student writing (a publication that is separate, by the way, from the college literary magazine). Such publications have cropped up on campuses across the country and succeed because they effectively tap a large, eager, and willing readership: the hundreds of students who enroll in composition classes each semester. What is new in our approach, however, is the idea of a peer-edited publication, as we have made *Choice Voice*. Instead of burdening faculty with the task of reading and judging submissions, we've created a student editorial board that reads and selects essays for publication. The board is composed entirely of students enrolled in first-year English and nominated by their instructors. Rather than loathing the editorial work, student editors embrace it and in the process seem to develop senses of identity and commitment that spawn lively, diverse, and always interesting editorial debate. One pleasantly unexpected result, as well, has been the number of *Choice Voice* editors who have changed their majors to English. Since we started publishing first-year writers on a peer-review basis in 1989, I've actually lost count.

During our first three years, we "published" *Choice Voice* by literally stapling dot-matrix printouts on two bulletin boards, one in the Writing Lab and one in the English department, where readers stood in the hallway and lingered over winning essays. Once we discovered how to publish *Choice Voice* electronically on the campus computer network, students started to read essays at terminals across campus. The trouble is minimal and the cost is nil. Instructors find it easy and useful to assign electronic reading assignments in the *Choice Voice* datafile, particularly during the invention stages of a writing project when students are most uncertain about essay possibilities, and it is most helpful to immerse them in a particular genre. Again and again, students say how much they learn from reading the work written by their peers.

The forms that publication can take are, of course, infinite. Most commonly, we turn to first-year English magazines, classroom anthologies, departmental newsletters, and campus newspapers, as well as books such as *Free Falling*. Essays in all of these formats can be distributed through the English department, circulated in local libraries, and placed in doctors' offices, bookstores, and coffeehouse reading racks. We also stage a *Choice Voice* reading each quarter where writers read their work to an audience of students, faculty, and administrators. We regularly draw a crowd of more than one hundred for noonday readings of first-year essays.

In the end, the principle behind publishing student writers is far more important than the form that publication takes. As sociolinguist John Gumperz points out: "Communication is a social activity requiring the coordinated efforts of two or more individuals. Mere talk to produce sentences, no matter how well formed or elegant, does not by itself constitute communication. Only when a *move* has elicited a *response* (italics mine) can we say communication is taking place" (1). In authentic written communication, writers write for readers who, by Gumperz's definition, create a genuinely communicative circuit: the move elicits a response. If we apply a linguistic model of language-acquisition to composition pedagogy, it is possible to argue that writers gain fluency, as speakers gain fluency, by negotiating membership in a discourse community. By creating the channel for writers to make conversational moves and responses, writing for publication establishes a social configuration that enables textual negotiation. The communicative circuit is genuine, rather than an exercise in writing "merely to produce sentences" or, as Britton says, to make a dummy run.

Publishing creates a discourse of authorship that is forward-looking. It leads students *toward* dialectic and dialogic possibilities rather than back into judgments about gaps, inadequacies, and knowledge deficiency. Publishing becomes a way of celebrating authorship and making tangible the value of the discourse act, most importantly, perhaps, because it makes students *want* to write. The surge of drafts that attends a student publication isn't quite a *tsunami*, but close.

Developing a writing-for-publication program in your classroom and composition curriculum is not a matter of finding an audience for student writing as much as it is a matter of creating that audience. The audience is, in fact, ready-made and consists of at least of those students enrolled each semester in first-year composition courses. The assumption that publishing means sending out manuscripts to journals, magazines, or newspapers may fit our professional model of publishing, but in the classroom this assumption restricts publication opportunities to the very few students who already think of themselves as writers. Journals, magazines, and newspapers are certainly viable avenues for students to explore and make submissions, but it's more productive to create a systemic channel where *all* students, including those less secure with their writing selves, can engage in communicative discourse through publication.

Choice Voice has visibly strengthened the sense of a discourse community for many writers at Augusta College, including instructors. It is interesting that, as student writing becomes authentically communicative, students perceive their rhetorical problems suddenly as genuine. The classroom attitude toward instruction noticeably shifts as teachers play with new coaching and support roles, creating a collaborative effect that contributes in subtle and important ways to the social and intellectual climate on campus. Thus, when their students get published, instructors celebrate themselves. And when instructors see things going right for a change, they generate fresh energy, not only in the classroom, but throughout the composition program.

A process-oriented publishing classroom provides a rhetorically situated model of composing where students engage in discourse that invites socially purposeful utterance and response and, thus, initiates them into the larger academic discourse community. Writing for publication is, in a sense, trial by fire, which is maybe why students so like it, and certainly why we need to do more of it.

Works Cited

Britton, James et al. *The Development of Writing Abilities* (pp. 11–18). London: Macmillan, 1975.

Gumperz, John. *Discourse Strategies.* Cambridge: Cambridge UP, 1982.

Mitchell, Ruth, and Mary Taylor. "The Integrating Perspective: An Audience-Response Model for Writing." *College English* 41 (1979): 247–71.

CHAPTER 2

REMEMBERING EVENTS

*W*riters *choose events to write about by looking to the immediate or distant past in their lives. Regardless of proximity, however, the techniques for telling the story don't change: the writer creates a dramatic present that weaves a pattern of significance using* external *details of time and space coupled with* internal *details of thought, feeling, and response. Of the essays in this chapter, two focus on events from adult life and three explore the more distant events of childhood. All, however, create vividly dramatic scenes into which readers can easily insert themselves.*

The title of Scott Weckerly's essay, "Free Falling," provides an intelligent framing device that doesn't begin to resonate with meaning until the metaphor appears in the final paragraph. Weckerly's subtle probing dramatically reveals the fear and uncertainty bound up in the event he writes about, the day he left home for college. The significance of this familiar event deepens as tension builds and readers move closer to the discovered truth that Weckerly reveals. In fact, the narrative's tension doesn't actually release us until the final word of the essay, when readers join the sky diver, take a deep breath, and jump.

From its humorous opening lines, Craig Anderson's essay, "Geothermal Holiday," hooks readers into a narrative quest camouflaged as a day trip to Ainsworth Hot Springs. The actual event is quite straightforwardly simple: they went, they bathed, they conquered. But the richness of the earthy metaphor that Anderson immerses his readers in endows the "actual" with an almost mythic significance. A vivid, present tense creates a scene with psychological immediacy that allows the writer to explore mysteries that are less than obvious in the experience. It is this exploration that bears significant thematic fruits.

In "The Relationship," Curtis Dean Adams displays a confident storytelling voice that subtly shifts its tone from wry humor to horror as events unfold, exposing the writer's own interior. In recounting the devastating effect of his father's murder, Adams is able to relate a painfully wrenching significance yet remain in full control of his material to the final sentence. Notice, in particular, how he keeps readers always close to a physical moment. Although the final four paragraphs of the essay sweep across fifteen years of experience, they do so by fully situating readers in concrete, and highly significant, specific places and events: an empty high school theater, a glance into a mirror, and, finally, an offstage wing during a performance of Hamlet. *Rather than tagging on a conclusion that resolves the essay by summarizing its significance or "moral," Adams skillfully maintains a narrative present anchored in a sequence of physical moments, enabling readers to experience and understand his meaning much more deeply.*

In "An Escape Journey," Abida Wali writes about her family's dramatic escape from their Afghani homeland. Like Adams, she rivets us with unfolding action in a close-up focus on an event: we read intently to find out "what happens." Also like Adams, she doesn't explain the significance *she's discovered but, instead, artfully renders it within the moment—in this case, when she arrives, crying, in Pakistan, "walking backwards to get one last glimpse of my beloved country." From this final powerful image, meaning resonates back through the narrative she's constructed.*

Finally, Richard Trenbeath's essay, "The Clean Zone," presents an interesting case study in form. He carefully renders a family universe with a rich circle of details that are layered with meaning so that they function as much more than simple details. It isn't until we're well into the scene that anything like an "event" even begins to transpire. And then we're deep into the event—the driving lesson with Gramps's truck—before the significance begins to subtly emerge. Notice that when the truck flips, so does the essay. The writer suddenly bursts with emotional longing to "undo the damage and start all over again." Like both Wali and Adams, Trenbeath doesn't announce his point or its significance. He simply weaves it into the fabric of the moment, showing readers how the action itself separated him from the past that he imagined. In the end, the writer re-creates the feeling of being "fixed" in a kind of eternal unworthiness, unable to escape the Clean Zone as he struggles to enter adulthood.

After reading these essays about remembered events, check yourself to see if you don't feel a yearning to turn back and read them again, not only for their rich authenticity, but also for how they "fix" you in their own Clean Zone, one that, perhaps, you'd rather not escape.

FREE FALLING

Scott Weckerly

•

Southern Illinois University
Carbondale, Illinois

Τhe impact of saying good-bye and actually leaving did not   1
hit me until the day of my departure. Its strength woke me an hour before my alarm clock would, as for the last time Missy, my golden re-
triever, greeted me with a big, sloppy lick. I hated it when she did that,
but that day I welcomed her with open arms. I petted her with long,
slow strokes, and her sad eyes gazed into mine. Her coat felt more silky
than usual. Of course, I did not notice any of these qualities until that
day, which made me all the more sad about leaving her.

The entire day was like that: a powerful awakening of whom and   2
what I would truly miss. I became sentimental about saying good-bye
to many people I had taken for granted—the regulars who came into
the restaurant where I worked, the ones I never seemed to find time to
speak with. I had to leave all of my friends and also the classmates I had
always intended to "get to know someday." Most importantly, I would
be forced to say farewell to the ones who raised me.

All at once, the glorious hype about becoming independent and   3
free became my sole, scary reality. I began to feel the pressure of all my
big talk about being a big shot going to a big-time school. Big deal. I
had waited so impatiently for the day to arrive, and now that it finally
had, I felt as if I did not want to go. I suppose that goes with the territory of enrolling in a university six hours from home.

Upon my decision to do so, in fact, all of my personal problems   4 had seemed to fade. I didn't care; I was leaving. I wanted to make it clear to everyone that I *wanted* to go—and by God, I was ready. Then the day came, and I wondered if I was honestly ready to go.

My dad and stepmom were taking me to school, but first I had to 5 say good-bye to my mom. No one ever said divorce was easy. I met Mom for brunch that morning, and she immediately began talking of my future experiences. More so, she talked a little of her first year away from home—cluttered dorm, shy roommate, some art history classes—and she spoke with such detail and enthusiasm that I clearly saw what a lasting impression college makes. We talked then of my expectations—what the guys on my floor would be like, how I hoped my classes would not be on opposite sides of campus, whether I'd gain weight on cafeteria food.

She paused for a second, and then quipped, "The food won't 6 make you gain weight; the beer will."

I smiled. I felt relieved that Mom was in a cheerful mood, rather 7 than a maudlin one. Ironically, the sky was filled with sunshine and bright, silky clouds. Somehow, I'd expected it to be gray and overcast. As we talked, I realized I would soon begin the long, complicated road to independence. The security I had selfishly taken for granted at home would eventually diminish into memory. Home would no longer be home, but Carbondale, Illinois.

When the waitress brought our bill, Mom's mood shifted no- 8 ticeably. She became quiet, even somber. I suppose for her that some-how signalled the conclusion of our last meal together, at least the last one for quite some time. She looked down at the table pensively. Look-ing back now, I can see the significance that day probably had for my mother. As a parent, she must have been anticipating that day ever since November 30, 1971, and it surely challenged her emotionally.

She walked me to my car, and I could feel my sadness in the pit 9 of my stomach. The summer breeze dried my eyes, and I blinked pro-fusely to moisten them.

"Well, I guess I have to go," I mumbled, looking into the distance. 10 I could not believe I did not have the courage to say that directly into her eyes.

"I know," she replied with a faint smile and then quipped, "It's 11 not too late to change your mind." She was joking, but there seemed to be some seriousness in her voice. Her smile quickly faded when I said I couldn't.

"I'm going to miss you," she added. 12

"You make it sound as if you're never going to see me again." 13

"You could call . . . collect, of course." 14

I laughed. The implication that all money spent from then on 15
would be my own was scary, yet funny as well.

"Don't worry about me too much, Mom." 16

"I'll miss you." She drew me close and gave me a hug, and I as- 17
sured her I'd be back sooner than she'd realize. She then told me that
she loved me.

"I . . . love you, too." The difficulty of saying those words over- 18
whelmed me. I had always seen myself as someone with solid, un-
touchable emotions. At that moment, though, I was in a fragile, quiv-
ering state; and I could not believe I had conjured such a false image of
myself.

We drew apart, and I slowly climbed into my gray Maxima. She 19
did not cry, but who knows what happened when I turned the corner.
I don't think I want to know.

At that time, I felt like a rookie sky diver preparing for his first 20
plunge. The cabin door opens to reveal the extreme distance of his fall,
which leads to either sheer excitement or eventual death. The näiveté
that sheltered his fear disappears at the sudden reality of the moment.
By then, of course, it is much too late to turn back. The very thought
that this was *his* idea seems absurd to him, and he feels like the only person on the face of the planet. And so he closes his eyes, takes a deep
breath, and jumps.

GEOTHERMAL HOLIDAY

Craig Anderson

•

North Idaho College
Coeur d'Alene, Idaho

Are you carrying any fruit or handguns?"   1

"Sure, I've got three kilos of kiwis in the trunk, and she has a .44   2
magnum in her purse."

No, that's not what I say to the border guard. It's best not to joke   3
with these guys. They don't have much of a sense of humor, and they
like to tear cars apart. Border guards make me nervous. I feel better as
soon as I'm beyond those expressionless eyes and frozen faces.

But a trip to Ainsworth is worth facing a hundred border guards.   4
Ainsworth Hot Springs. I've been wanting to go for years now. Everyone I know has been there. It's gotten to the point where I feel deprived
whenever anyone starts talking about Ainsworth. So off my friend Margaret and I go on a cold, rainy November Tuesday—not a bad day for
hot springing.

A few miles into Canada the road changes. It winds along Koote-   5
nai Lake for fifty miles with only about three spots for cars to pass the
whole way. I've never seen a stretch of highway with more curves.
Kootenai Lake is dramatic, mountains rising sharply from this narrow,
hundred-mile slab of gray. Rustic, privately run campgrounds, closed
for the season, dot the roadside every few miles. Our destination is the
Kootenai Ferry, which the Canadian government runs to the other
side of the lake every hour, free of charge.

We're the last car to board. Nautical looking workers in navy blue   6

16

direct us to a parking space on the lower deck. We climb steep stairs to the passenger level. The wind and rain gain intensity as the ferry pulls away from the dock and heads across the lake. I step outside on the deck, but only for a minute. The rain slashes sideways, driving me back inside under an awning I try to use for cover. The ferry is starting to sway. Margaret tells a story of a ferry ride she once took from Sicily to Malta when she got seasick from diesel fumes and waves. Some kids are running toy cars up and down the plastic seats. Through rain-mottled windows the mountaintops are obscured in mist.

Soon we're pulling into the dock on the far side. Cars file off the ferry, and we head the last nine miles to the hot springs. Admission is $4.00 Canadian. There aren't any lockers; each of us gets a plastic bag to put our clothes in, which we check with a clerk who gives out velcro wristbands with claim numbers on them. Mine is 38. Rain dots my body as I head out to the pool. The big pool is warm—a good place to get psyched-up for the hotter pool above and the caves. The caves! That's what makes Ainsworth so unique. We paddle back into the mountainside following the hot water to its source. Dim lights reveal an incredible scene. The walls are seeping hot mineral water. The minerals have built up over the years to form strange, whitish stalagmites in a million shapes. The farther in we wade, the hotter it gets. At the very back of the cave, a little hot stream flows out of the rocks. In this chamber, even the air is hot, like a sauna.

Floating in the mineral water back in that cave, I get a powerful sense that the Earth is alive. I can feel the energy surging right out of the planet. I feel as though I'm in the womb of Mother Earth, basking in embryonic bliss. She soothes and nurtures me. She's beneficent. After all, she could crush me with the slightest shrug. But she doesn't. I wonder if the Indians felt the same way when they named this place "paradise"? According to the story, they discovered the hot spring by following deer who came here to heal their wounds. Now here we are, doing the same.

All of a sudden I'm just too hot. I've got to get back outside. I let the current take me toward the daylight. Emerging from the cave, I feel as though I'm being reborn. The cool rain is a relief. I lounge in the pool, looking at Kootenai Lake far below. A cold, rainy day can be beautiful from the vantage point of a hot spring.

Hours seem to pass. We chat with other visitors: hot springs bring disparate people together. One old couple is talking in Swedish, or maybe it's Russian. A little kid finally gets up enough nerve to go into the cave with his mother. Some guy says he liked it better before

7

8

9

10

they put the lights in. Time is crawling. Relaxation is a hard thing to measure, but this might be a personal record.

Finally we've had all the water therapy we can take. I feel (and 11 look) like a sponge. But I have to go back into the caves one more time before we leave. I tour the dim passages again, running my hands along the wild-shaped, seeping walls. I'm an Indian. The Earth is my Mother. Earth whispers, "I'm not an inanimate object. I'm alive! Listen. I speak if you listen. I speak with warm water, fresh breezes, glorious sunsets, and good food. How could I say it any better?" I drift in a primal ceremony, giving thanks for the ancient mysteries still left in the world. The cave mouth gives birth once more to a human reawakened to Earth-power.

Maybe we won't destroy this planet after all. Maybe we're not as 12 powerful as we think. I give the Earth a fighting chance. We might destroy ourselves. The Earth will survive.

The homeward journey flows smoothly, like the hot spring from 13 the cave. Yes, now I can say I've been to Ainsworth.

"Are you carrying any fruit or handguns?" 14

"No," I answer. "I have nothing to declare." 15

THE RELATIONSHIP

Curtis Dean Adams

∎

Augusta College
Augusta, Georgia

> *Revenge his foul and most unnatural murder.*
> —William Shakespeare, *Hamlet*

$\mathbf{A}$s the new year of 1973 approached, I was a thirteen-year-old boy living in an ugly brown-and-white aluminum mobile home attached to a huge, highway safety–yellow fireworks store. It was surrounded by twelve miles of stinking swamps and saltwater marshes; these were infested with mosquitoes, wild boars, and alligators. Man, I was happy. I had my dog, my books, a semiautomatic .22 rifle with a telescopic sight, and access to enough explosives to blow up a small country. To most other boys my age, mine was an enviable position. As eldest child, and only boy, I also enjoyed the privilege and solace of wandering through the swamps whenever the spirit moved me.

We had been living in the swamps for a year and a half. From the suburbs of Augusta, my father relocated us to this smelly, low-country wasteland (whose major crops were methane and poisonous snakes). The reason for the move was financial. We would be fleecing Yankees on their yearly migrations to and from Florida. This, it turned out, was easily accomplished by selling them an endless variety of tacky items: fireworks, pecan rolls, sexist beach towels, life-size rubber snakes, tapestries of dogs playing poker, and velvet paintings of either Elvis or Jesus. (I'm not sure who was more popular.)

Our store was named Crazy Cecil's, although my father's name was not Cecil, and he wasn't crazy. It was huge, brightly-lit, and packed to overflowing with worthless items. Like flies drawn to garbage, peo-

1

2

3

19

ple stopped at our store and couldn't seem to help themselves. We raked in so much of their money that we soon opened two more stores on the same deserted stretch of Highway 17.

But our prosperity and our troubles were soon received in equal measure. Evidently, because our stores were the biggest and the tackiest, we were running our local competition out of business. And, understandably, our local competitors were not enthusiastic about the trend continuing. I discovered this when, in late November, I woke to the sounds of cussing and falling boxes. I ran through the dark trailer and into the store as my father finished extinguishing a burning stack of boxes filled with moccasins.

"What happened?"

"Somebody threw a bomb through the window."

"Why?"

"To blow us up, damn-it; now go see to your mother."

I stared in amazement.

"Move boy!" my father shouted.

I moved, since I knew it wasn't smart to make my father repeat a command. I found my mother, face in hands, in their bedroom.

"Why would someone want to kill us?" I asked.

"Honey," she said softly, "we're making lots of money here. Before we came here other people were making that money."

"Like the Tylers," I said matter-of-factly.

The Tylers, none of whom I had met, were a family who owned a much smaller store a few miles up the highway. Having built newer stores on either side of them, we were slowly squeezing the life out of the Tylers' business.

Slow on the uptake, I would never be a detective. "You mean the Tylers did this?"

"Yes, I'm sure they must have," Mom said. She was looking at me with a calm, sad pity in her eyes that I didn't understand.

I was mad and ready to fight. "Why did they do it?"

"Honey, I'm sure the Tylers would like us to leave, so they could make the money they were making before we came."

"Well, that's too bad," I said.

"Yes," she said, "and I'm certain your hardheaded father feels the same way."

The funny thing is, it took the police six hours to show up that night. I sensed that something wasn't right.

The next day, my father told me that we had been quite lucky. The "bomb," a Molotov cocktail, was a bottle of gasoline with a gas-

4

5

6

7

8

9

10

11

12

13

14

15

16

17

18

19

20

21

22

23

soaked rag tied around the neck for a fuse. As the bottle came through the window, the lighted rag caught on the glass and slipped off the bottle. "Had it not," my father informed me, "son, we wouldn't be having this little talk."

While my father seemed worried by this turn of events, I was not. I had faith in my father's ability to handle any situation. 24

An imposing figure, my father stood well over six feet. His jet 25 black hair and red beard, though neatly trimmed, gave him the look of a pirate. His green eyes burned with the fire of a man who had sold his soul and wanted to get his money's worth before the bill came due. Large-boned and muscular, he was built like a linebacker, yet he moved with the smoothness of the high school basketball player he had been at one time. He was big, good-looking, and as slick as boiled okra, and he knew it.

My father had also been in the army for a brief time and served 26 as a sergeant in an armored unit. Like the biggest dog on the street, Curtis Senior loved a face-off. In 1972, the phrase "I'm sorry, but you can't smoke here" was virtually unknown. Now and then, when my father would spot some large, mean-looking man smoking in the store, he would tell me, "Watch this." And, with a huge cigar clenched in his teeth, my father would slowly stride over to the man in question and say, "You can't smoke in here."

The man in question would look at him incredulously and say, 27 "You're smokin', " at which point I could smell testosterone from fifty feet away.

"My store," Dad would say. 28

Then they would glare at each other for a few timeless seconds, 29 and my father would smile his slow smile as the man of the day, sometimes cussing, sometimes not, would finally put his cigarette out on the floor. For my father, the youngest of six boys from a dirt-poor Kentucky family, that sort of head-butting was what he thought of as a good time.

Then, on New Year's Eve, 1972, my father faced off with some- 30 one who wasn't as inclined to back down.

On that New Year's Eve, I was outside among the large, yellow 31 billboards and flashing lights on the road, playing with an assortment of loose fireworks. It was cool that night but not brisk. The swamps were dormant, and the stench of a paper mill hung in the air.

SWISSTH . . . CRACK! SWISSTH . . . CRACK! Bottle rockets flew into 32 the air. Depending on the accuracy of the fuse, I was able to come within a few feet of cars traveling the highway a hundred yards away, although

I had stopped targeting cars a few months before when one of my targets turned out to be a state patrol cruiser.

SWISSTH . . . CRACK! 33

A couple of weeks before that New Year's, as we hurried to open 34 our third store, Looney Luke's, a second firebombing occurred. But because the new store hadn't been stocked yet, and because my father possessed the foresight to use a double-wide fireproof mobile home as a building, the fire caused little damage. We simply repainted, stocked the shelves, and were ready for the New Year's rush. "That'll show those stupid sandlappers," my father had said, pleased with the lack of damage.

SWISSTH . . . CRACK! 35

SWISSTH . . . CRACK! I looked at my watch—two hours till the new 36 year. My father was at the other store, and I wondered what was going on there—seven miles down the road. I thought about the bomb threat we had received that very evening.

SWISSTH . . . CRACK! 37

"Dean! Dean!" My mother called to me from the store, her voice 38 thin, cracked, urgent. I ran into my nightmare.

Inside the trailer, I found my younger sisters, Robin and Ginger, 39 ages eight and seven, wailing uncontrollably as my mother fumbled with their clothing. Toni, age ten, was already dressed. She stood blank-faced as if someone had stolen her brain. My mother's face quivered, as if it were ready to explode into a million pieces.

"The hospital called. Your father's been shot," she said, her voice 40 skirting the edge of hysteria. She might as well have slapped me full force across the face.

"Is he all right?" I asked, barely managing to pull the question 41 from my mouth.

"They won't say over the phone. They want us to come down." 42

That was when someone stole my brain. 43

My mother loaded us into the station wagon and drove her cargo 44 of quiet, stunned children south, down Highway 17 toward Savannah.

We arrived at the hospital emergency entrance. Dazed, I floated 45 in with the rest of the family. As we entered the hospital, one nurse took our mother from us as another sat us down. We were quiet, still in shock. Two or ten minutes later, I can't remember, a nurse led us down a sterile tunnel to a large, empty, dimly lit, gray-tiled room. There stood our mother and two nurses. One of the nurses had her eyes fixed on mine. I could tell she was about to speak.

"Your father is dead," she said. 46

My mouth opened, and I took in every ounce of air in that room 47
with a sound no child should be able to make; the nurse opened her
arms, and I fell in. With the exhalation of my breath, my soul became
a river of sound and tears. That nurse wrapped her arms around me with
the strength of steel straps on a powder keg.

I must have cried myself out, because after that night, I didn't shed 48
another tear for two days, until, at the surreal, open-casket wake, I
thought I saw my father breathe and had to be taken, screaming, from
the room.

When we got home from the hospital, a flock of detectives were 49
waiting for us. They explained that my father had been killed by a bullet from a high-powered rifle while he and his partner were standing in
the parking lot of the newest store. The assassins had been parked across
the highway in a black Cadillac, and they were gone before my dad's
partner could figure out how to switch the rifle he was carrying off the
safety position. The detectives said it had been a professional job.

A black Cadillac? 50

Hired assassins? 51

Had we been propelled into the television world? 52

The detectives wanted us to pack quickly so they could move us 53
to a motel where they felt we would be safer.

"I need a gun," I said, starting for my father's pistols. 54

"No," said my mother in a quiet but firm voice. 55

"Yes," I said, matching her tone. And I meant it. 56

"Son," someone said, "there's no need for that. If these people 57
want you dead, you're dead."

Very comforting words. 58

We left Savannah the next day in a chartered plane bound for 59
Kentucky.

At Slate Hill Baptist Church, we buried my father's body on a high 60
hill overlooking the now snow-covered, rolling pastures of the south-
eastern Kentucky landscape. It seemed the perfect place to be buried.
London, Kentucky, the hometown of my father, mother, and myself.
Those hills had some inexplicable hold on my soul, maybe because
"our people" had lived there since the country's first push westward.

The weather was ideal that day: cold, overcast, with large 61
snowflakes falling slowly to the ground. As I followed too closely behind the dark suits carrying my father's casket to the grave, I felt my
mother's hand on my shoulder pulling me back to her. I recalled that
while she was in college, her father had been murdered in a chance encounter with an escaped convict. She knew the drill.

That day I had thought my relationship with my father was over. 62
I was a presumptuous thirteen-year-old.

A few days after the funeral, I remembered sitting under a pecan 63
tree at school, six months before his murder, as a friend told me about
his own father's death in a motorcycle accident and how the event had
ripped his life apart. I had thought about my relationship with my father, and on that day, I had determined that if my father died, it wouldn't
be a big deal. Wrong again.

My father's murder stole my sanity as well as the sanity of my en- 64
tire family. Our house became a zoo without a keeper. Our mother
opened a restaurant and had to work countless hours every week, leaving her four children ample time at home to scream and fight in our
wild frustration. Toni locked herself in her bedroom for a period of five
years and was rarely seen leaving it except to attend her Evangelic Baptist Church. I wanted to be more help to my family, but I was too
angry, too bitter, and too wild—an animal trapped and gnawing off my
leg to get free from the trap. I couldn't stop feeling my father's eyes
upon me. I begged my mother to send me to a military academy for
eighth grade; my soul screamed for order. But I was able to find no escape in a uniform; my storm was internal, and I couldn't run away from
myself or my father.

His ghost haunted me in various ways for years: nightmares, fear 65
that kept me sleeping with a gun under my pillow, disapproval I perceived in the eyes of adult men. I would dream of his return, his walking through the door saying, "Why haven't you avenged my murder?"
It was in the houses of my fellow teenage friends that I was most uncomfortable; I saw my father's disapproval in their fathers' eyes.

In my senior year of high school, the theater found me, and there 66
I found some diversion from my inner turmoil. Around three o'clock
in the morning, in an empty theater, while working on a lighting design, I had just related something about my father's nasty temper when
my friend Gershon, looking down at me from a twenty-five-foot lad-
der, said, "You didn't like your father very much, did you?" At that moment, Gershon fired a diamond bullet and placed it square between my
eyes. I had not liked my father when I was thirteen, but, I had thought,
what boy does? His murder had relieved the tension of misunder-
standing between us. I had been glad he was gone all those years, allowing me to become (however screwed-up) who I was. This hidden
guilt had been my chain.

And that marked the beginning of the healing. It was ten years 67
after his murder that Gershon's truth began to scrape the scales from

my eyes. Many difficult years and conflicting emotions lay ahead. Now, more than twenty years after his death, wondering what form our relationship would have taken were he still alive, I look in the morning mirror and give a wry smile as I notice the blue eyes my mother gave me slowly turning into the green of my father's.

Standing in the wings during a recent production of *Hamlet*, I shuddered hearing Hamlet tell his father's ghost what I would tell mine: "Rest, rest, perturbed spirit!"

68

AN ESCAPE JOURNEY

Abida Wali

■

University of California, San Diego
La Jolla, California

It was 11:30 P.M. in Kabul. We were all waiting for my uncle 1
to return from a meeting with his collaborators. Every night before the
curfew, they distributed *Shabnameh (The Night Letter)*, a pamphlet
mimeographed or copied by hand and secretly left in public places.
Many people had been arrested, tortured, imprisoned, and killed for the
possession or distribution of antiregime *Night Letters*. Usually, my uncle
got home by ten, but now the clock was about to strike twelve midnight.
What could have happened? Had he been arrested? If he didn't get
home before the midnight curfew went into effect, he could be shot.

Suddenly, a pounding at the door broke the silence. My heart beat 2
faster and faster as I rushed to the door. Who could it be? Could it be
my uncle—or soldiers coming to arrest my dad after they arrested my
uncle?

"Who is it?" I asked. 3

"Open the door," a voice replied from the other side of the door. 4
I didn't recognize the voice.

"Open the door," the voice repeated. 5

As I turned the knob, the person pushed the door open, throw- 6
ing me back against the wall. My uncle rushed into the living room. I
slammed the door and ran after him. Trembling and gasping, he looked
toward my dad and said "Abdulla and Ahmed have been arrested . . .
they could have given my name under torture . . . I'm next."

26

"We have to leave immediately," my dad replied.   7

I helped my mom pack canned foods, clothing, and the first aid   8
kit. We were told to take only the things that we would need for our
journey, but Mom slipped the family photo album between the clothes.
After a frantic hour of rushing from room to room, gathering our sup-
plies in bundles, we had to wait until the curfew was lifted at dawn. At
the crack of dawn, we abandoned the house forever, setting out on an
uncertain journey. As Mom shut the front door, she looked for the last
time at her great-grandmother's teapot.

We took a bus from Kabul to Nangarhar. Along the road to Nan-   9
garhar were two or three checkpoints where soldiers would search the
bus for arms and illegal documents. At the first checkpoint, a soldier
got on the bus. From the hammer and sickle on his cap, I knew he was
Russian. He wore a big army coat and held a rifle, an AK-47 Kalash-
nikov, to his chest. His boots shook and rattled the windows and the
metal floor of the bus. Suddenly, he stopped, pointed his gun at a man,
and signaled him to get off the bus. The man ignored him. The soldier
stepped forward and tried to pull him out of the seat, but the man clung
to the seat and wouldn't let go. My heart was racing. Drops of sweat
were forming on my forehead. Finally, the man let go and was escorted
by two other soldiers to a jeep parked beside the bus. The pounding of
the boots against the bus floor started again, and this time, the soldier
stopped at my dad and me.

"Where are you going?" he asked.   10

"To my uncle's funeral in Nangarhar," Dad answered.   11

"Your ID?"   12

Dad gave him his ID. The soldier opened it to see the picture. I 13
felt a drop of sweat drop from my forehead. Finally, the soldier handed
back the ID. He looked around the bus once more and gave the driver
permission to pass.

We made the rest of the journey in fear of getting blown up by   14
antipersonnel mines. I saw six passenger buses that had been destroyed
by mines on the road to Nangarhar. Finally, after eight hours of traveling, which should have been four, we reached Nangarhar.

From the bus station we took a taxi to a friend's house and waited 15
there two days for someone to smuggle us across the border. After two
days, my dad's friend introduced us to the Smuggler. His six-foot height,
bushy beard, upturned moustache, and dark eyebrows made him look
dreadful. He wore baggy trousers and heavy red-leather slippers with
upturned toes, and he had a carbine slung over his back. He was a
Pathan. The Pathans, an Afghan ethnic group, are warriors who obey

neither God nor man. Their law is the law of the rifle and the knife. He told us that he could take only three or four people at a time. My parents decided that I should go with my aunt and uncle.

We had to dress like the Pathan peasants who lived near the border, so that our western clothes did not advertise the fact that we were from the capital and trying to escape. My uncle dressed like the Smuggler. My aunt and I were given dresses with colorful patterns and sequins (which made the dresses very heavy) and dangling jewelry. In addition, outside the city, the women were obliged to wear a Chaderi, a veil through which we could see but not be seen. It comes in three colors: yellowish brown, gray, and blue. Ours were yellowish brown. [16]

We left the house at dawn and walked a mile or two to reach the main road. While walking, the Chaderi twisted and clung to my legs. As I looked down to unwrap it, I stumbled over a rock and fell to the ground, injuring my right knee slightly. It burned, but I managed to catch up with my aunt and uncle and acted like nothing had happened. After a short time, a lorry arrived for us, and we spent the next few hours with sheep and goats, covering our faces with a piece of cloth to keep the smell and the dust out. [17]

The sound of a helicopter approaching got our attention. It was an MI-24, a kind of armored helicopter that the Russians used to bombard villages, agricultural fields, and mosques. We feared that this time we might be its target, but fortunately it passed us. After a few minutes, we came upon a village. From a small opening in the side of the lorry, I witnessed the aftermath of a bombardment. The air attack had reduced the village to rubble, and those who survived it were running around shouting and screaming. An agricultural field outside the village was burned to ashes, and a pall of smoke and dust drifted over the valley. The images of those people and their ruined village haunted us the rest of our journey. [18]

After a few hours, the lorry stopped, and the driver opened the gate and called, "Last stop." Holding the Chaderi, I jumped to the ground. The desert was covered with the tracks of horses, donkeys, camels, and people. There were many groups of people traveling in caravans: young orphaned boys; a lonely man with a sad expression on his face, all of his possessions packed on top of a camel; and numerous donkeys carrying women while their husbands walked alongside. We were all on our way to Pakistan. [19]

As we waited for our donkeys, my uncle whispered to me: "The Smuggler is a government agent, a Militia." My heart skipped a beat. I knew exactly what that meant—he would turn us in. The government [20] recruits tribesmen like the Smuggler for undercover assignments. The Smuggler was talking with some other people, looking at us as he spoke. When he started to walk toward us, I thought my life was over. I wanted to scream and run. He stopped and signaled my uncle to come. As they walked toward a mud hut in the distance, my whole life flashed in front of my eyes. I saw my school, my parents, my execution.

"Did they take him for interrogation?" I asked myself. I could see the hut, and I wondered what was going on inside. When my uncle came out the door, I ran to him. He had been bargaining for the price of the mules. We rented four mules and set out with the caravan. 21

Riding that mule was an experience that I will never forget. It was hard to stay balanced with the heavy dress and the veil, especially once we began to climb a mountain. The trail was just wide enough for the mule to put down his hooves. As we turned and twisted along the mountainside, I wondered whether I should close my eyes, to try to shut out the danger, or keep them open, to be prepared when we fell down the side of the mountain. But the mule was surefooted, and I didn't fall. I learned that if I could relax, I would not fall off. 22

It was a hot summer day, and I became thirsty. The sun was right above our heads, and my thirst became intolerable. My mouth was completely dry. We could see a village at the bottom of the mountain — four hours away, according to the Smuggler. After a few minutes, however, we got to a small lake. The water was yellow and covered with algae, but the Smuggler drank it and brought me a cup of water to drink. As I looked into the cup, I was reminded of the solution that we prepared in biology class in order to grow bacteria. This was the main source of water for the village. God knows what microorganisms were swimming in that lake. 23

"I wouldn't drink it if I were you," my aunt said. 24

But I closed my eyes and drank the whole cup at once. I would worry about the consequences later. 25

We reached the village just before sunset. After eating dinner and resting for several hours, we started to travel again. The night journey was magnificent. The sky was clear, the moon was full, and millions of stars seemed to be winking at the night travelers. We could hear the bells of another caravan coming from the opposite direction, getting louder and louder as it got close. The ding-a-ling of that caravan added a rhythm to the lonely desert. 26

Now we were in the territory of the Freedom Fighters. We knew if they recognized the Smuggler, they would execute all of us as communist spies. The Freedom Fighters and the Militia are enemies, and 27 the Freedom Fighters did not trust anyone who was traveling with an agent.

At dawn we reached a small teahouse. It consisted of a large, bare 28 room with a dirt floor covered by canvas mats. A few small windows, with plastic in place of glass, let in a bit of light. A smoky wood fire in a tin stove served for heating and boiling water for tea. The owner brought us tea and bread, a soothing sight for restless travelers.

We walked on, and soon a signpost got my attention. As I got 29 closer, I was able to read the words: Welcome to Pakistan.

I started to cry, walking backwards to get one last glimpse of my 30 beloved country.

THE CLEAN ZONE

Richard Trenbeath

•

Augusta College
Augusta, Georgia

I still recall the sensations of entering my grandparents' house. 1
Carefully opening the side door where two outside walls meet to form
an L, I step in, taste the heavy earthen dampness rising from the black-
ened cellar opening and, with some apprehension, close the door. In
near darkness, I turn a sharp left and bound three steep steps as quickly
as I can. Holding my breath so as not to look panicked, I open the next
door to the safety of the kitchen. It is there, within the first inch of security, that memories of growing up and of childhood flood back so
strongly.

The kitchen was known as the Clean Zone. Like the rest of the 2
house it was tediously clean but smelled curiously of older folks. Full
of food canisters and appliances, utensils and pots of every kind, the
kitchen was a standard for measuring a grandchild's worth. By heeding
the barked instructions, "Check your tops and bottoms twice," we kids
had permission to cross over the edge, Grandma's invisible kitchen line
separating brown, grass-stained tennis shoes and dirty elbows from
everything scrubbed white. On the other side of the Clean Zone, past
the empty hallway and hidden behind a heavily draped glass door, lay
my favorite place.

It was my goal each morning after pre-breakfast chores to be 3
properly inspected at the invisible kitchen line, cross the Clean Zone
without harm and make it to the glass door. Slowly turning the cut crys-

31

tal knob to catch the changing light was like finding a secret code that unlocked the barrier. On the other side, a whole other world took form, completely separated from the rest of life. I walked in it Indianlike, as if in an unknown forest. Each thoughtful step on the large carpet slowly crushed the thick wool pile, causing it to speak back in faint cracking sounds. Each deep sample of breath would be the same as the first one, smelling strangely of objects never moved and sweet with the resins of carved African woods. My grandparents' living room served as a family museum. In one sweep of wall, from sunken bookcases to the corner, I could scan a century's worth of relatives. There, two men balanced on large sticks protruding from the base of a giant red tree, above a forest of smaller trees, pushed and pulled at each other from the ends of a very long saw that was only half as wide as the red tree's base. On a small table were cold marble elephants and black carved birds stretched exotically thin and slender, their necks and heads nearly touching in a tall spiraled embrace. The trunk that I dared to open was probably my Uncle Robert's, a missionary in Africa. Thinking of the mysteries linked to the indecipherable carvings on that thick crest, and breathing ever so shallowly so as not to be poisoned by the strong vapors inside, I let it miraculously take me to the dark continent, to Kenya where my cousin Lloyd, who was also eleven, nearly lost his sight from a snake bite.

In that limitless expanse, I imagined faraway places and traveled 4 along centuries as I examined old worn faces and ancient steam-driven farm tractors. I crossed a universe of time to touch, see, and smell my past, my family, my history, and came to know things spoken of only by the older ones. Here I freely traveled, knowing things. I never kept track of time in the museum, although one morning I did. It was the morning Gramps was going to the farm and said he would let me drive the old Ford again.

That morning I barely let myself travel half a century through the 5 living-room museum before it was time to leave for Uncle Jack's, Gramps's old farm. When we arrived, Gramps parked next to the machine shed instead of by the house as usual. Next to us was the dull green 1949 Ford pickup, drooping on the edges from years of labor, sitting in its usual parking place at the end of the wooden sidewalk, where I used to overhaul it when I was so small it took me three tries just to jump up on the running boards. Gramps would sacrifice the Ford, his faithful traveling companion, so I could jack it up and change the radiator water twenty times in a morning, thinking I was doing him a favor. The truck still smelled the same, sort of like old cigars, old dirt, and old truck, the same smell it had years ago when my older cousins were being taught how to drive. Back then, Gramps either didn't know the danger he was in, or else he liked having one of them in mock control of the Ford, his excitement for the week.

Now it was just Gramps and me. The 9 A.M. sun smudged its way through layers of dust and greasy-rag trails on the never-washed windscreen, burning right into my eyeballs. Eyes squinting half shut, I sat behind the wheel studying the enameled dials with their colored pointers, the large, cold steering wheel, the pads of flat rubber mounted on long arcs of metal that disappeared through holes in the floorboards — clutch, brake, throttle, shift-rod. The whole shift assembly stood half as tall as me. When Gramps explained the small white starter button, I realized I was putting complete trust in him. With the button depressed, the old Ford, locomotive-like, shook and breathed to life.

I needed Gramps's strong left hand over mine to help force the shift-rod to its proper slot, and I needed his vision against the sun to see beyond the engine cover. Undaunted, Gramps raised one arm and dropped it, wagon master style, cigar pointing to the desired direction of adventure. The narrow path south of the house and between the two woods gave me a chance to see where I was piloting the noisy pile of loose bones until the sun surprised us again where the path intersected with the main gravel road. Here the coolies reached right up to the edge of the tire marks, filled from recent rains and loud with croaking frogs and water bugs, topped green with islands of moving stuff. Gramps's cigar pointed right, but I hauled the large, black steering wheel to the left. With a jump and a jolt from the clutch pedal (which snapped loose again), the back end of the truck began to spit a large left-hand arc of gravel faster than the front two tires could dig one up. That put us high and dry, going left, perfectly between the wet parts. I never did tell Gramps that the wind came through his window just at that moment and placed his cigar ashes in my eyes right along with the dirt that flew from my violent clutch action. Nor did I tell him that I never saw the road. I was just hanging on for all my eleven-years' worth.

During that final driving lesson, a tingle of pride surfaced. I knew I had measured up to Gramps's expectations, just like my older cousins before me, because I was given my first big work assignment. After I steered the old Ford to Gramps's house, he got out and left me on my own. My pride was measured by a broad grin, I remember, when I realized I had mastered the clutch pedal. The trick was to let it out slowly, not all at once. I felt older, grown up, like a teenager allowed in the Clean Zone without reminders to inspect my tops and bottoms.

It was just past the grain elevators that the old 1949 Ford started 9
its routine, a sway to the left then back to the right, a motion for which
I must have overcompensated. One moment I was sliding right, hands
anchoring me to the steering wheel, and the next I was sliding left
against the door, stomach instantly sensing danger, sick and dizzy from
each slide, fearing the worst. One moment the truck was on the right
shoulder of the road; the next it swung to the left shoulder; then, without warning, it screeched all the way around, rear tire catching a clump
of tall sod, and I was cartwheeling, around and around a hundred times
without control, my arms and legs trying to touch something. The
noise was deafening and confusing. Each flat side of the truck met the
earth with a loud, hollow, metallic whump. The odd collection of machinery parts that were under the seat beat against the metal insides of
the truck like hail. I remember hearing someone screaming over and
over again, "Stop! Stop!" But I couldn't. I was too sick inside, weak and
scared. I could only hang on until, finally, my body lay in a jumble of
noise, truck wrong side down.

The first person to respond to the disaster was my cousin Kent. 10
Still sick and shaking, I couldn't look at the truck nor at Kent, feeling
somehow ashamed that I had mucked up the family tradition. I didn't
hear a word Kent said. I heard only my own thoughts and anxiety: how
could I undo the damage and how could I start all over again? Too, the
lump in my throat, like the tightness one gets from shouting, hurt so
much that I didn't think I could talk. When Gramps arrived I couldn't
face him either. Head down, overflowing with embarrassment, I pretended I didn't notice him. Gramps lowered himself along the ditch,
surveying the damage with half of Neche, North Dakota, milling
around him and his mortally wounded traveling companion, the old
1949 Ford. He glanced my way and instinctively I pretended to be
looking at the ground, feeling bad for disappointing him. Without my
noticing, Gramps climbed out of the ditch and stood next to me. Star-
tled and caught off guard, I looked right at him. His eyes were soft,
showing no anger, only a glint of knowing all about overturned trucks,
perhaps from his own past, or maybe from my father's or my cousins'
past. He said, "Well, now we know what she looks like on her top." And
that was that, no more was ever said about it.

Even though he never mentioned the crash, the few minutes' ride 11
from the spot where the old Ford lay close to death and my grandparents' house seemed agonizingly long and silent. I wanted to escape, to
be alone. I wanted to be in a different place where nobody knew me, in
another time far off from everyone else, like an unknown traveler in the

museum. Once back in the house, across the Clean Zone and in my grandparents' living room, I found that I had to force myself to travel from mystery to mystery, from Africa to the forest of the big red trees. Traveling was neither easy nor natural anymore. I just couldn't feel the freedom. The collection of photographs in the museum stared back at me coldly that day, and, really, from that point on they were just old pictures of people nobody knew anymore. I couldn't open the chest whose special vapors took me to the dark continent because I knew it wasn't mine to touch. I didn't have permission to explore. Looking through the windows toward the woods wasn't like looking to another place in time anymore. The thought that I was in my grandparents' living room and that the woods were just fifty feet away bound me tightly to reality. No more was I a traveler free to move at will; escape was impossible. Thoughts of who I was seemed to smother me. Was I fixed in time? Was my story in this room somewhere, propped behind other insignificant old pictures for other strangers' gazes? In the shame of being a youngster measured against an adult world and feeling the failure and depression of the present, I slowly turned my back on the museum. As I closed the draped door behind me, I instinctively raised my feet, checking my bottoms twice, before entering the Clean Zone, hoping I'd be worthy.

CHAPTER 3

REMEMBERING PEOPLE

*W*riting about people often transforms them. When we put someone on the page, that person doesn't, of course, become literally different, just differently understood. Close examination unearths surprise and reveals dimensions of the subject (and ourselves) that otherwise remain hidden and perhaps unknown. The four essays in this chapter are remarkable because none of them settles for easy or facile surface description. All four probe, reflect, and examine more deeply the patterns that reveal the human personality and soul, those layers of ourselves and others that rarely show up on first glance.

Hope Goldberg weaves memory and reflection into a rich pattern that unveils the interior of her childhood dance teacher by presenting the details of her exterior—speech, appearance, manners, actions. Notice how subtly Goldberg brings herself onto the page, as well, blending Gail's life with her own in that final image of the cookie cutter that reveals the thread of significance the writer seeks: in this image, two lives, no longer separate, become one.

Erick Young uses a technique similar to Goldberg's, capturing the external details of manner and speech to present an incredibly vivid portrait of Mrs. K, also a former teacher. Young, too, brings himself onto the page and subtly immerses Mrs. K in the context of their student-teacher relationship. The rich portrait that emerges is the product of the writer's quiet and careful examination of his subject, exactly the kind of "writerly" move that Mrs. K, ironically, would have expected.

Samuel Jeffries skillfully weaves moments of his own life with moments of his father's life. In his willingness to go beyond easy description, Jeffries trains his eye on the less available interior of his father, and unearths dimensions of the man that, if not hidden, are at least not obvious on the surface. Through his description of the parenting that he received as a child as well as the parenting he would someday like to give as an adult, Jeffries creates a subtle chain that leads to his speculation on the parenting his father received. This essay forges so deeply through *the past in its journey that it is surprising when it arrives full circle at the very place it started—the moment of the candles on the writer's fifth birthday cake.*

Although Todd, Jeffries's father, is clearly the "remembered person" in this essay, notice how the writer's focus on their relationship allows the writer to emerge artfully on the page without jarring readers into feeling that the topic has shifted. By the end of the essay, it becomes more than apparent that the writer has discovered something about both his father and himself. Perhaps Samuel Jeffries's own words in his conclusion express the value that writing can have as a means of self-exploration and discovery: "Only now . . . am I able to make full sense of the grumpy toddler in the photograph, and reconstruct for myself that small piece of my childhood."

Margaret Zenk displays a similar willingness to go beyond the simple surface as she links a remembered person, her mother, into a larger pattern of meaning that has quite a different shape. For Zenk, the pattern she discovers lies beyond the psychological interior that so intently occupies Jeffries. By exploring the broader social context of her mother's past and present, Zenk is able to illuminate and more sharply clarify her subject. Against the backdrop of this larger social universe, Zenk describes how her mother has affected her own life, and, in doing so, subtly reveals the path they share through the dense forest of cultural assumptions about gender. Notice how both Zenk and Jeffries, in their two essays that focus on a parent, are able to get so much from their writing, far more than what we might expect from such a deceptively simple assignment—remembering a person.

GAIL

Hope Goldberg

•

University of Cincinnati
Cincinnati, Ohio

She used to make toe-shoe cookies and hand them out after dance class from a tin that had been used Christmas after Christmas. Never mind that everyone else made cookies in the shapes of Christmas trees or stars. Her Christmas toe-shoe cookies had pink icing where the satin and ribbons went, and she even used little gold candy balls to decorate the tip of the slipper, the part you would stand on if your feet had been inside those cookies. The instep was shaped perfectly (as she would have shaped all our feet), probably because she made the cookie cutter herself and had free creative license with the design. "Have a cookie," she would offer, "but only one . . . you look like you've put on a couple of pounds." She would smile generously as we filed past, one by one, taking our single cookie ration. She, of course, could eat pasta, cookies, all sorts of fattening things and never gain an ounce. And she did. Constantly.

At fifty-plus years old, she was five foot two and weighed a mere ninety-four pounds. Her body was like a sixteen-year-old's, and, were it not for her slightly wrinkled skin and graying blonde hair, she could easily have passed for a teenager.

Gail and her husband, Walter, lived with Gail's mother— "Mummy," she used to call her. I considered this one of her artistic affectations, like calling Walter "Darling" and the way she pursed her lips to kiss the air between one's cheek and ear when greeting a person.

These seemed appropriate remnants of her glamorous performing career. Her home was filled with relics and autographed photos of famous dancers. "To Gail, with Love, George" was scrawled on a picture of Balanchine taken in the 1930s. Her life was spread out in dance symbols from one end of the house to the other. It seemed to me such a fantasy, a marvelous and unusual and exotic life. She often invited me to visit her, which always made me feel special and honored. "Shhh," she sometimes whispered as I entered. "Mummy's sleeping. She hasn't been feeling well lately." I nodded my head in agreement, not daring to make a sound until we had moved silently into another room to talk. In one fluid movement, she scooped up Suki, the youngest of her beloved Siamese cats, then stroked her as long as Suki would allow. "Did I ever tell you about the time I worked with Danny Kaye at Radio City Music Hall?" she asked, her eyes focusing dreamily into the distance as she reminisced. "He was delightful to work with, a very smart and funny man. . . ." I absorbed these stories with a mixture of wonder and envy. Her life began to take on epic proportions during these sessions. She had been a dancer all her life, and to my young eyes she was everything I wanted to be. I listened and imagined myself on those stages with Balanchine, Tallchief, Fonteyn.

In class she was relentless. "You have to force the turnout," she would demand. "Close the fifth. Tighter!" She had come from a generation of dancers for whom sacrifice and pain were the badges of honor, and suffering for one's art was the ultimate reward for ambition. We accepted this, silently and courageously, as we did all her criticisms. "Anissa," she yelled, "from the waist up you really look like a dancer. You have great feeling." I was crushed because this meant to me that I obviously did not look like a dancer from the waist down. I wondered how I could possibly have lived this long being only half of what I so longed to be. I hated my short, heavy legs, so unlike those in the pictures of New York City Ballet dancers on the walls of Gail's house. Those were the standards by which we were judged. I'm sure to this day that she meant to be nice, but half-good, half-murderous compliments were a regular occurrence in our classes. Thank God I wasn't the heaviest dancer in the class and that I had some redeeming qualities in her eyes. I had feeling. I just had to pound my body into submission. And I knew I could do it.

When I was about thirteen and needed to dance every day to become a professional, Gail gave me a work/scholarship because my parents couldn't afford tuition. This meant I had to help clean the studio (I had seen Gail push the big dust mop around the studio floor a million times, so I knew that part) and demonstrate for the beginning classes. She would tell me secrets about teaching: "You have to let the little ones have fun," she confided. "You've got to get them hooked on ballet" (she would place the accent on the first syllable, BAL-let) "before you can make them work hard. They have to like it first. If you work them too hard, you'll lose them." I nodded in agreement, realizing that I probably would have had them slaving at technique and would have surely lost all of them.

Once I asked her why she and Walter didn't have children. It 6 seemed strange to me (having come from a family of five kids) that she should be childless. "I've never wanted any children," she replied with total candor. "I have all of you, what would I want with children of my own? Just a lot of diapers and mess. I've got so much to do; I'm much too busy." It was true: there was choreography to create, classes to prepare, music to select, costumes to design, paperwork to complete—Gail ran a business, took care of her aging mother and emphysemic husband. And all of us. We were her world.

When I was sixteen, Gail coached me for a major part in *Cin-* 7 *derella*. We spent hours alone in the studio, working on every detail of interpretation. "Slowly . . ." she coaxed, "gently. That's it. . . . Don't rush the music. . . . Let it lead you into the arabesque, yes, that's it. . . . Beautiful, Anissa!" I could feel her reach deep inside of me, drawing out my best performance with a sensitive combination of encouragement and criticism. Near the end of these rehearsals, Gail gave me a book on ballet terminology that she had carefully copied by hand in ink when she was very young. She had even copied the drawings of body positions and facings, how to hold one's hands, one's fingers, one's head. Every detail had been meticulously reproduced. She had kept it all her life, and now she was giving it to me. "I want you to have this," she said, pressing the book into my hands firmly, "and some day you will pass it on to one of your students, too."

Years later, when I started my own ballet school, I was determined 8 to encourage my students toward a whole life. "You must go to college," I insisted. "There is a world other than dance." I gave them gifts from my heart—love, support, encouragement—but at Christmastime, without fail, my students' favorite gifts were the toe-shoe cookies with pink icing and gold candy balls I made with Gail's handmade cookie cutter.

ONLY SHE

Erick Young

.

University of California, San Diego
La Jolla, California

Those eyes. Brown. No no, deep, dark brown. Hardly a wrin- 1
kle around them. Soft, smooth skin. And those eyebrows. Neither thick
nor thin, just bold—two curves punctuating her facial expressions with
a certain something. Surprise, amusement—up would shoot one of the
brows, the right one I believe, just slightly, accompanied by a mischievous little smirk. Anger, irritation—up and inward shot both brows,
tightly pressed, followed by a sharp "What d'ya want? Don't bother
me!" She never really meant it, though; it was just her way of saying
hello. Even though she wore glasses she could still see all, with or without them. Her deep, dark brown eyes were no ordinary eyes; no, within
those deep wells rested a pair of magic orbs, two miniature crystal balls
that could peer into your mind and read all your little thoughts. Some
thought she had psychic powers. She knew what you were thinking, or
at least she always seemed to know what I was thinking, even my most
complex, inexplicable thoughts. And that was all that seemed to matter
at the time. Only she, only Sonia Koujakian, Mrs. K.

I do not recall the first time I noticed her at school, but Mrs. K 2
was not one to blend into a crowd. I would see her walking briskly across
the school rotunda, tall and lean, wearing a skirt and a mauve-colored
raincoat, holding a stuffed beige handbag in one hand, and a bright red
coffeepot in the other. She seemed so confident, always looking straight
ahead as she walked about school. Perhaps it was her hair that first

caught my eye. It was short, a mix of light brown and gray, combed slightly up—almost spiked. Not the typical sort of hairstyle for an English teacher at our school. It set her apart and made her look dynamic. Already I knew that she was somebody special.

The PSAT brought her into my life for the first time, in my sophomore year. Even though she was the senior English teacher, she offered to coach any undaunted sophomores or juniors after school for the nefarious "SAT jr." Trying to be the savvy student, I joined a small group who gathered in her cove after school to practice vocabulary drills and sentence completions. Mrs. K would scold us on the finer points of grammar, giving us her "come on, get with the production" look as we reviewed our errors. Not the typical reaction from a teacher; she treated us like peers and would say to us whatever was on her mind without pretense, pleasantry, or euphemism. We could do the same, if we had the guts to try. Her casual disposition made me feel both relaxed and nervous; none of us knew how to act around her, whether to joke and tease her, or respect and honor her. We all agreed, however, that she was as down-to-earth as they come. Two years later, as an older and wiser senior, I would get a full dose of Mrs. K's personality.

My first day in Mrs. K's class left much to be desired. I entered to find most of my classmates just laughing and joking. The first-day-of-school jitters had become passé, and the smugness that comes with seniordom dominated the room. It was a convention of Alfred E. Neumans, and the nonchalant air of "What Me Worry?" filled the classroom. Some students, however, sat very quietly. These were the wise ones; they'd heard about Mrs. K. Academic tensions hovered like the inevitable black storm cloud above Room 5C3. There was a small fear of the unknown and the unexpected nudging about in my stomach as I sat at the far end of the center table. Strange how this was the only classroom in the entire building to have six huge wooden tables instead of forty individual little desks; someone must have wanted it that way. For once I was not too anxious to sit up front. Suddenly the chattering diminished. Mrs. K was coming.

In she ambled, with her stuffed handbag and bright red coffeepot, wearing a skirt and the mauve raincoat; she was just as I had remembered. She scanned the room, and up went her right eyebrow. A most peculiar "I-know-what-you-are-up-to" smirk was our first greeting. Now I was nervous.

"All right ladies and gentlemen, I want to see if you belong in my class," she began. "Take out a pen and lots of paper." Pause. "Now don't get too worried over this, since you are all geniuses anyway. You know, if you've got it you've got it, if you don't. . . ." She shrugged. Pause. "Some of you know you don't really belong in here," she chided, pointing her finger, "and it's time you stopped getting put in Honors English just because you passed some silly little test in second grade. Well now we're going to see what you can do. Okay now, stop and think for a moment, and get those creative juices going. I want you to write me a paper telling me the origin of the English language. You can be as creative as you want. Make up something if you have to—two cavemen grunting at each other, I don't care. You have until the end of the period. Go."

It was not the most encouraging welcome. For a moment the whole class just sort of slumped in their seats, drained suddenly of all vitality and hopes of a relaxed senior year. Blank faces abounded, mine included. I had no idea what to write. The origin of the English language? Being "creative" seemed too risky. What ever happened to the good ol' five-paragraph essay with specific examples? Well I didn't have any specific examples anyway. I remember staring at a sheet of white paper, then scrawling down some incoherent mumbo-jumbo. I wanted to impress her, too much. "It was nice knowing you," I sighed as I handed in my paper. What a first day. 7

Fortunately, that first day with Mrs. K would not be my last. Although the class size shrunk over the following days as some students ran for their academic lives, I was not prepared to leave. I knew Mrs. K's class would be an arduous English journey, but I could never let myself miss it. It would be a journey well worth taking. 8

As the weeks continued, tidbits of Mrs. K's colorful past and philosophy about life would somehow always creep into lectures and class discussions. We found out she had served as a volunteer nurse in a combat hospital in Japan and had "seen it all—even grown men cry." During the 1960s a wilder Mrs. K could be seen cruising the streets of San Francisco on motorcycle, decked out in long spiked boots and short spiked hair. She later traded in her motorcycle and boots for a Fiat and white Reeboks. And there was a running joke about her age. Mrs. K could not be much less than forty-five, but just as Jack Benny was forever thirty-nine, she was forever twenty-eight. One of her T-shirts said so. Twenty-eight was a good year, she would tell us, but she never quite explained why. 9

I would come to deeply trust and respect this eccentric lady. I guess I have *Oedipus Rex* to thank for our first out-of-class meeting. We had to compose an extensive essay on the Oedipus trilogy, on which much of our semester grade would be based. Foolishly, I chose to write 10 on the most abstract topic, predestination and divine justice. I toiled for days, torturing myself trying to come up with some definitive conclusions. Finally, I realized my struggle was merely carrying my mind farther and farther adrift in a sea of confusion. I needed someone to rescue me; I needed Mrs. K.

We arranged to meet in the Faculty Commons, a small, smoky room of teachers with red pens at work and administrators shooting the breeze over lunch. I crept inside with notes in hand and took a seat. She soon arrived, holding a tuna-on-wheat, a chocolate chip cookie, and the red coffeepot. "I hope you don't mind if I eat while we talk," she said, "but if you do, I'm going to eat anyway." Smile. 11

We talked the whole lunch period. I felt awkward at first, actually struggling to explain *why* I'd been struggling with the assignment. But then Mrs. K the Mentor emerged—soft spoken, introspective, wise. I opened up to her. We sat beside each other at that table, reflecting on predestination, divine justice, and life. A ray of sunshine cut through clouds of confusion. Our reflections were interrupted by the lunch bell, but we continued later after school. Two days and two drafts later, I had gained more than just a deep understanding of Oedipus Rex: I had gained a friend. What was it about this woman that enabled me to reveal a different part of myself? Never before had I spoken so openly about my thoughts, or about myself. Most people did not understand my cares and thoughts. But she understood. 12

I would go back to Room 5C3 many afternoons later to sort my thoughts. To her I was no longer Erick but Hamlet, because of my pensive and complex nature. "Okay Hamlet, what's on your mind?" our conversations would begin. Every writing assignment became an excuse to spend time after school talking and reflecting, me at the wooden table, her at her stool. We digressed on everything from *Paradise Lost* to Shakespeare to "The Road Not Taken." Sometimes other students would come for help on their papers, and I would always let them go first, so that I could be the last left. Often I would learn about more than just literature: "Life's not black and white, it's a hazy gray, and you've always got to use that wonderful piece of machinery God gave you and question things because nothing is clear-cut." I noticed my perceptions changing, as well as my writing style. More of my character entered my writing, and the Mr. Detached Impartiality persona I once favored faded into the background. Being "creative" no longer seemed risky. She told me to put more of myself into my creations, and I listened. 13

One afternoon near the end of my senior year, I asked her about her favorite novel. "Oh, without a doubt, *Les Misérables*," she replied. 14

"But I never could find an unedited version." On Graduation Day, in a sea of seniors hugging one another, red-and-blue mortarboards sailing through the air, I searched through the crowd for Mrs. K and handed her a small box. Inside with a long thank-you on the cover was a new copy of *Les Misérables,* unedited and unabridged.

I doubt that I will come across many others like Mrs. K. Only she   15
would sit with me one-on-one, and review every minute detail of a draft. Only she would give up an afternoon just to shoot the breeze. Only she could I call a mentor, a confidant, and a friend. I still think of Mrs. K. Sometimes, when the pressures of college come crashing down, and the order of life seems to have run amok, I go to my room and slowly close the door and my eyes, sit down, and talk with Mrs. K.

"Okay Hamlet, what's on your mind. . . ."   16

CANDLES

Samuel Jeffries

▪

Brown University
Providence, Rhode Island

M y mother spent my fifth birthday in jail. She and and her 1
friends had taken part in a No Nukes rally at a local power plant the
day before, fully aware that they would end up spending the night in
police custody. To some people, missing a child's birthday may sound
terrible, or at least like something not to be easily forgiven, but I hold
no grudge against her. Truthfully, I don't even know how I felt about
it at the time, as memory becomes stubborn and uncooperative when
asked to reach back so far into the past. All I have as a record of the moment is a color photograph. It shows a plump-faced boy standing in a
yard, wearing a large, sour pout. Behind him on a card table sits what
looks like a round, flat cornbread. This was the un-iced cake that my
father made for an improvised birthday celebration. Even though I
can't remember the scene, I can imagine what it must have been like.

At the time of my birth, my parents were renting a small cabin 2
deep in rural Vermont. In order to make the monthly $180 payments
on the "Little Brown House," as they fondly called it, my father worked
as a carpenter and my mother a midwife. I have seen pictures of them:
my father had a thin, scraggly beard reaching down below his chest, and
my mother's straight, dark hair fell to her waist. Because my parents separated soon after my birth, I find the idea of their living together more
difficult to imagine than anything else about their lives.

My strongest impressions of my mother are of her ambition, her 3
frankness, her confidence. We have never really discussed my fifth
birthday, but I can easily picture her sitting down with me beforehand,
clasping my small hand in hers and explaining, plainly and warmly, that
although she wouldn't be at my party, it didn't mean that she didn't love
me. "You're my Little Bear," she would have said with a sincere smile,
"and you'll always come first in my heart, even though the things I do
might not always show that."

For my father, on the other hand, words like those would not 4
come so easily. Todd, as I knew my father when I was growing up, was
a child's perfect companion: he took me on long walks in the woods,
invented intricate scenarios for my entertainment, and filled our hours
together with ongoing jokes that only we shared. Outside of his sheltered world, even today, my father often seems reserved, even awkward.
When I introduce him to people who have heard my glowing descriptions of his wit and intelligence, I am frustrated by how little of the man
comes through in the bland, lifeless persona he wears around strangers.
Todd's passive approach to life must have conflicted directly with my
mother's need for action and control. She could only have been frustrated by her husband's reluctance to emerge from the spare nest of security he had gathered around him.

When whatever mystical bond that held my parents together fi- 5
nally dissolved, my mother and I moved down to northern Virginia.
After a few months had passed, Todd followed, out of devotion to me,
and it was then that my life as I now know it began.

I am told that I fought my father's first attempts to spend time 6
with me. When he would come to pick me up for a visit, I would cower
in my mother's arms and sob with the full force of a child's tantrum.
Even after I began to spend the weekends with him, it was a long time
before I felt completely at ease—I can still feel in my stomach the
plunging homesickness of those Friday and Saturday nights. For Todd,
this must have been both confusing and painful to endure. He is not
one of those men who casually absorbs any emotional missile thrown
his way or deflects such attacks with one bold sweep of an armor-clad
forearm. Such fathers are the stuff of television, and, once in a great
while, the alien homes of school friends and playmates. The man whom
I grew up calling by his first name, and only recently trained myself to
address awkwardly as "Dad," does not often reveal his emotions to others, but neither does he easily conceal how the difficult times of his life
have challenged and, ultimately, transformed him.

One recent summer evening, after one of his famous meals of   7
whole-wheat pasta and homegrown salad greens, my father began to talk
about his childhood in small-town Pennsylvania. Todd's youth is one
of his favorite subjects; detailing past experiences and friendships, he
seems almost reborn with the exaltation of reminiscence. Visiting him
now in his small, single-story house, I don't need to watch him pace ex-
citedly around the kitchen spouting animated tales of his boyhood to
know how lonely he is.

Todd's family had been prominent in the city of Pottstown, and   8
his descriptions of life in a sprawling home with its well-kept lawn have
often reminded me very much of the episodes of *Leave It to Beaver* we
watch together with ironic fascination. To me, such a life seems as un-
real as the black-and-white tones of the TV show suggest. I have grown
up in the aftermath of a divorce, and a constant fluctuation between two
opposite poles of adulthood is all I know. Both my parents were, in their
own contrasting ways, strong and loving. What strikes me now is how
genuine they seem as people. It is as though they didn't have time to
play the traditional adult roles, and instead related to me on an infor-
mal, personal level that has become my model for parenthood. When
I see the great emotional chasm separating many of my friends from
their parents, I am grateful to have grown up not with a pair of unap-
proachable elders, but with two great adult friends.

My father, however, was raised in a home steeped in respect and   9
the mask of good cheer. To be sure, his family was every bit as healthy
as mine, and the love he shared with his parents was genuine. The family took constant care, however, to maintain an image of prosperity and
happiness for the rest of the world to admire. The resulting sense of security must have been strong. As a boy, my father had never imagined
that things could be any different than they were, that there could ever
exist any other notion of a good childhood than his own.

It was only with the passing of time that he came to rebel against   10
this standard, seeking to redefine his place in society like so many of his
generation. Hitchhiking across the country, bound to one place and job
only until the restless tugs of boredom set in, my father, my mother,
and their friends struggled to break free of the veneer that had coated
the relationships they had grown up with. This mission was still very
central to my parents' lives at the time of my birth; rather than re-create
in the candlelit and incensed Little Brown House a replica of the
Cleavers' suburban Eden, they went instead to what seems like the opposite extreme.

By the time I reached the age at which Todd had been building   11
model cars and playing Little League, not even television dared present too rigid a vision of the "typical" family lifestyle. This did little to
put my father's mind at ease, however. To see his son shuttled back and
forth between two homes and two sets of clothing violated his instinct
toward a nuclear-family environment. Whereas Todd's home had been
dominated by the bold breadwinner who strode through the door every
evening at five o'clock, thinking only of dinner and a glass of Scotch, I
knew my dad solely from Saturday strolls in the woods and his one-man
puppet shows. Despite his successful efforts to leave the facade of his
childhood behind, the ideals he had been raised with proved unshak-
able.

"I worried," he told me there in the moist Virginia night, "that   12
you didn't even see me as a father at all, but more as just some guy, like
an uncle or something." This was a revelation to me: all those years of
my boyhood, Todd had been concerned that I wasn't growing up right,
that I was missing something vital in the development of a complete,
healthy child. It didn't matter that the two-household arrangement was
to me perfectly natural; my father resented being left out of my growing up, and was plagued by doubts about how to best raise a son whom
he saw only two days out of the week.

With his insecurities magnified by my reluctance to spend time   13
with him, Todd made sure that we never lacked things to do in our time
together. What I had seen as the unflagging energy of a unique and
wonderful mentor was motivated, at least in part, by my father's anxiety about how to fulfill his paternal role. To fit the unfamiliar shape of
our relationship, Todd had retooled the parental ideal of his youth into
a new model of involved, caring fatherhood. At the same time, he was
able to meet his obligation to himself, remaining true to the values of
responsibility and support that had mattered so deeply to his own father. It is comforting to realize that whatever kind of parent I eventually will become for my own children, these same enduring standards
will guide me, like an adult grasping a child's uncertain hands to mold
wet clay.

Only now, after the unique moment of connection we shared, am   14
I able to make full sense of the grumpy toddler in the photograph, and
reconstruct for myself that small piece of my childhood. Even when my
father disagreed with decisions my mother had made while raising me,
like joining the antinuke protest instead of throwing me a birthday
party, he always tried to make what he felt to be the right choices, ac-

cording to his basic principles of duty to a son. In the process, he gave me the best kind of parent any child, in any situation, could have hoped for.

"There's no map for parenthood," Todd said to me that night. "You just have to push ahead and do what you feel is right." It is with that phrase in mind that I can see him studying the unfamiliar instructions on a box of cake mix, then solemnly and painstakingly sinking five bright candles into the soft, warm crust.

15

DIFFERING WORLDVIEWS: MOM AND FEMINISM

Margaret Zenk

■

College of Saint Benedict
Saint Joseph, Minnesota

Over the past four months, my mother and I appear to have 1
developed a psychic connection. Every time I call home, she answers
the phone with, "Oh, Margie, I had a feeling you were going to call
today." This is especially impressive because, more often than not, I call
on the spur of the moment, for no reason at all. In the past few weeks,
her psychic abilities have expanded. When I mentioned having considered inviting my boyfriend and his mom to our house for Thanksgiving, she was delighted, having already considered that she ask me to invite them.

The psychic bond between me and my mom is, of course, more 2
a joke than anything. It does, however, serve as an example of how close
we are. We have similar builds (as Mom ruefully observes), similar
voices (even close relatives have trouble telling us apart on the phone),
similar hobbies, and similar values.

Psychic link or no, I have always been very close to Mom, telling 3
her little things about my day, borrowing books from her, revising papers for class with her, teasing her, and being teased. Even when I was
a teenager, Mom was my friend, which helped me gain a lot: an appre-
ciation of poetry, well-used semicolons, interesting mathematical
quirks, a love of working with my hands, an odd sense of humor. Most
importantly, though, my mother, because of the person she is, has
greatly influenced my attitudes toward my femininity.

Everyone on my mom's side of the family is, in the nicest possi- 4
ble way, amazingly conceited and competitive. She and her brothers and
sisters grew up hearing my grandpa's motto: "The cream rises!"
Whether they were male or female wasn't all that important: they were
Herzogs and thus, by definition, cream. This attitude can definitely be
taken too far, but it does have a positive side. In high school, one of my
teachers told the class that many women of her generation became
teachers, nurses, or secretaries simply because those were the only jobs
available to them. This never occurred to my mother.

When it was time for Mom to choose a major in college, she de- 5
cided to study math. Her reason was that math was something she was
good at but probably wouldn't pursue on her own, as she would literature or home economics. She took all of her math classes only from
the two chairs of the math department, because, she explains, she simply thought she deserved the best.

Even today, more men major in math than do women; twenty 6
years ago, this imbalance was much greater. Mom was always one of two
or three women in her math classes, and since her Herzog confidence
wasn't unrealistic, she was also near the top of each class. Under these
circumstances, it would be incredible if she hadn't experienced sexism
and discrimination; I'm sure her classes could not always have been
pleasant. Yet, Mom doesn't remember feeling uncomfortable in any of
them. In fact, she kind of enjoyed being in the minority, she says. Everyone knew her, she points out, and it wasn't a bad way to meet guys.

It is, I suppose, remotely possible that Mom was unbelievably 7
lucky and actually wasn't discriminated against. Far more likely, though,
is that not expecting to encounter sexism, she failed to recognize it.
Naive, perhaps, but whom did her naivete harm? Mom's lack of awareness seems to have effectively neutralized any discrimination she may
have experienced.

Mom's failure to recognize discrimination can hardly be consid- 8
ered a consequence of mere naivete, however, at least not over a span
of four years. Few people were then or now that oblivious to the attitudes and behaviors of people around them, and Mom certainly wasn't.
Rather, she lived according to different assumptions than did many
women of the 1970s. That she was as intelligent and as capable as a man,
she considered not only true, but beyond doubt. With this assumption,
she could explain slights that might otherwise have been classed auto-
matically as sexism. She called them personal differences, or ignored
them entirely.

As I grew up, I absorbed this worldview. My mom never seemed 9 to doubt that I was smart, possibly brilliant, so I didn't either. That I was limited in any way in the world because I was a girl simply never occurred to me, nor to my three younger brothers, at least not seriously. Granted, when we went camping, my brothers always insisted that building the fire was a boy's job, but that was only a clever way to escape doing dishes. I could build a fire just as well as they could, and I was, for years, the reigning pillow fight champion. If my brothers made the typical "I'm better because I'm a boy" comments as we grew up, it was more a way of teasing me, the only girl, than anything else; and they never got any support from my parents.

Both Mom and Dad have always contributed to the atmosphere   10 of equality at home. Far from being threatened by Mom's intelligence and accomplishments, Dad was proud of them. For the most part, Mom and Dad made decisions together, and household chores were shaped around practical, rather than gender, considerations. Being the first one home in the evenings, my mother usually cooked, but Dad cleaned up after dinner. While both of my parents are very traditional in many ways, I never heard anything described as "women's work" or "men's work." At bottom, though, a lot of my assumptions about gender equality can be traced to my mom. After all, who could take seriously the idea of women being in any way inferior to men, with a mother who insisted that she was perfect?

I do not claim that the world is perfect. It is an undeniable fact   11 that women are not treated equally in our society. Science, government, and management classes on college campuses are dominated by men even today. Women are paid less than men for equal work, and they find it harder than men to advance past middle-management positions in many businesses. Sexual harassment is, despite increasing awareness of the problem, still a menace in the workplace. I am aware of all of these problems and wouldn't dream of denying their importance; but the issues of feminism remain for me, as for Mom, largely intellectual concerns, remote from my own life. As I grew up, I never had to struggle to be seen as equal to a man; I just was. Even now that I am aware of the inequality in our society, it is hard for me to believe that anyone could seriously consider me to be in any way inferior to a man.

Mom never joined any of the feminist demonstrations of the   12 1970s. She never burned her bra, refused to shave her legs, protested. Instead, she chose a major in which she was always one of three or four women in a class full of men, and she excelled in it. Instead, she raised four children for whom the idea of gender equality is so obvious that arguing about it seems silly. By viewing the world as one in which her equality was beyond dispute, she avoided much of the rhetoric and activism of the feminist movement while living out the core of the movement's goals.

When she was in college, one of Mom's favorite songs was Helen 13 Reddy's "I Am Woman," with its memorable line "hear me roar." Mom may not have had a great deal to do with the feminist movement and may not have much patience with the sense of women as victims of discrimination, but she agrees wholeheartedly with basic feminist principles. She may follow these principles in unusual ways, but as she recently pointed out, there's more than one way to roar.

CHAPTER 4

WRITING PROFILES

*W*hen a piece of writing has immediacy, readers become transfixed, locked onto the page, "in the gaze." When a profile has immediacy—and the good ones always do—the event, person, or place seems to unfold before our eyes. In this respect, a profile writer resembles an Action-Cam reporter on television news: on the scene to capture the intensity and detail of the moment. The writer is the camera, in a sense. As you read the essays in this chapter, notice how each exposes the lesser known, the unpredictable, the surprising, even the quirky dimensions of its subject. Look for what it is that "hooks" you and holds you to the page.

The use of the present tense in his essay, "Bullseye," helps Drew Long deliver the Automatic Amusement Bullshooters Darts Tournament directly into the reader's dormitory or living room. In his vivid rendering of the barroom atmosphere, Long follows the tournament's progress with a carefully balanced presentation of concrete physical detail and necessary factual information. Notice that the result is a crisp pacing that engages the reader's interest and creates a feeling of "being there." Also notice how Long offers his profile from a participant's perspective. Because of his direct involvement, he is able to offer the reader a window into the subject that would be otherwise unavailable, particularly if he used information solely gathered from interviews with those who did participate. Another reason for Long's success in the essay is the strong, confident voice he is able to project. See if you can detect how his language and point of view create a voice on the page that seems to be talking out loud.

Perhaps the best introduction to Todd Hoffman's profile, "Interview with a Marine Sniper," is the question he poses in his conclusion: "How many people really know what . . . goes on in a war?" His answer is demonstrated in a gripping profile of an unusual and, as he points out, hardly stereotypical government job— that of the U.S. Marine sniper. As with Drew Long's essay, an important dimension of Hoffman's essay is the captivating voice he establishes and the *language he uses to do so — a distinct combination of euphemism and precise abstraction. The result is a forward-driving tension that keeps readers turning pages. His statement, for instance, that "the primary function of a sniper is to eliminate as many key targets as possible" hardly belies the risk, drama, and violence of the act being described. Yet, such abstraction accurately renders the language of military personnel who must, of necessity, objectify their mission and erase from consciousness (to the degree that this is possible) the risk, drama, and violence of their jobs. By the end of this profile, Hoffman makes clear how soldiers factually, yet, he suggests, reluctantly, embrace the mechanisms and objectives of warfare.*

Linda Kampel's essay, "Our Daily Bread," profiles a soup kitchen that, at first glance, would seem to present nothing out of the ordinary. Yet, as Kampel says in her opening, walking into this place is "like stepping into a different world." It is the purpose of her profile to engage readers in discovering this world, one they likely are familiar with yet perhaps have never visited. Notice how Kampel capitalizes on the strategy of "entrance" into this world to convey for readers an interesting sense of commonality as well as difference. Kampel alternates between descriptions of setting and of people to blend effectively the unfamiliar and the familiar. She keeps readers interested by presenting surprising new information, while at the same time she lets readers feel comfortably connected to the people who are so crucial to her subject. Establishing this common ground of connection with readers by using a "human-interest" focus is a highly successful strategy. Another strength in this essay is the way Kampel effectively weaves her own observations and responses with the quotations she gathered from her interviews with others. This skillful blend of the personal and factual allows her to narrow the distance between herself and her subject. Subsequently, that distance is narrowed for readers, as well. Instead of a purely factual profile, Kampel's "Our Daily Bread" bears the stamp of the writer's distinct personality.

Melanie Papenfuss approaches her profile, "Behind the Sugar Curtain," by following the flow of time on one particular evening during the sugar beet harvest. She creates a strong narrative anticipation that illustrates one solution to a problem all profile writers face: how to present factual information without slowing the pace to a plod. One of Papenfuss's techniques is, literally, the question. Notice how she continually poses questions that provoke short answers condensed in dialogue to retain dramatic immediacy in the lightning-quick pace of speech and, at the same time, remaining thoroughly informative.

BULLSEYE

Drew Long

■

Hawkeye Community College
Waterloo, Iowa

T he sights, the smells, the sounds. A lovely bouquet of flow- 1
ers. The sweet fragrance of perfume. Classical music caressing your
eardrum.

You definitely will not find these things at an Automatic Amuse- 2
ment Bullshooters Darts Tournament. What you will find are rows and
rows of automatic dartboards. The smell of beer and cigarettes. The
constant pounding of jukebox music assaulting you from every side.

The flyer says the games will start at one o'clock on Saturday, 3
since the weekends are usually the best days to hold these tournaments.
We show up thirty minutes early to get a table close to a dartboard. A
few dartaholics are already there, warming up. Looking down at them,
I'm amazed at the many variations of darts that they use. A dart has three
main parts: the tip, which sticks into the board; the shaft; and the flight,
or "feathered" part, which guides the dart through the air. Watching
these players throw, I see darts with white, black, and blue tips. Darts
with multicolored flights, some striped, some with pictures. A scorpion
over here, even the American flag. There are chrome shafts, metal
shafts, and rubber shafts. Six-inch darts and three-inch darts. Darts
weighing nine grams up to darts weighing twenty grams. It is a kalei-
doscope of traveling projectiles.

"The biggest problem I faced when setting up this tournament 4
was advertising," tournament director Eric Rohm tells me as I catch him

in a rare moment of peace, "Most people won't see the flyer unless it's placed right beside the coin slot on the dartboards. That's one problem. Plus, my darts get stolen a lot," he adds with a scowl.

Eric loves to throw darts. For many a year he has hiked up to the throwing line, concentrated on the bullseye, and smacked it with his darts time after time after time. Eric makes no money from directing these tournaments (unless, of course, he wins the tournament), since all entry fees are paid back out to winners as prize money. Without a profit motive, Eric say he organizes and sponsors darts tournaments because he loves the game. As for his darts getting stolen, it's my hypothesis that people steal them hoping Eric will do poorly without his darts. 5

He doesn't, however. 6

"The games to be played today are a 501 singles tournament, a cricket singles tournament, and Luck of the Draw cricket," Eric told me as I paid to get into the games. "Luck of the Draw is a random tournament. Once everybody has signed up, I let fate decide who plays with whom. Two people are on each team, and they play another team, competing for the best two out of three games of cricket. The winners move into the winners' bracket; the losers move down to the losers' bracket. Double elimination; last team to win all its games is the champion. We'll do Luck of the Draw first." 7

Getting my darts out to practice, I walk up to an empty board. This wonderful, magnificent invention of modern electronics stands almost nine feet tall and about two feet wide. The actual throwing area is approximately five and a half feet up from the ground, a towering monstrosity that blocks the sun if placed too close to a window. 8

These are soft-tip boards, which are easier to keep score with, plus, the darts are not as dangerous to throw as those with hard, metal tips. I'm sure that most bar owners don't want drunk patrons armed with metal-tipped darts getting into fights. The soft tips, made of a firm plastic, are rounded at the end to stick in the numerous small holes that crater the dartboard, while the metal tips are pointed at the end, which makes it easier for them to embed themselves in the cork dartboards that are common in homes and offices today. 9

Eric informs me who my partner is. I get extremely lucky and draw Jo-Jo to accompany me through the mystical journey called team cricket. Like Eric, Jo-Jo is a dart master. We're set to play. To win at cricket, our team must close out numbers fifteen through twenty, plus the bullseye, and be either tied for or have the most total points. To close a number, we must get three marks in it, which we can accomplish by hitting either the single area (one mark), the double area (two 10 marks), or the triple area (three marks). Points are scored by hitting a number that our team has closed but the other team hasn't.

Interestingly enough, cricket comes from the Old French word 11 *criquet*, which means "a bat used in a ballgame," and has nothing at all to do with darts. Why there is a dart game named after a bat or a bug will remain a timeless mystery.

Stress runs high as the dart games begin. There are several ex- 12 cellent dart players in this tournament, and, while others tell me that I'm good, I know that I'm up against tough competition with these peo- ple. Most of them have been playing for several years and probably have the time to practice every day.

Even with all the competition, Jo-Jo and I get off to a great start. 13 Winning our first three matches, we're set to play in the championship match. Never before have I advanced this far in a tournament.

As I sit bathing in nervousness thinking about this final champi- 14 onship game, I hear some woman scream from across the room, "On the board! Did you just start playing this game yesterday?!" Apparently, the partner she is paired with had missed the board and hit the black region around it, a result which gives you no marks or points. This voice repeatedly echoes during the course of the tournament. I guess that ei- ther a lot of people are missing the board, or she's just obnoxious.

It's not hard to get hooked at throwing darts. There's something 15 alluring about that bullseye, drawing people to it again and again. All types of people get into darts, from the hard-nosed businessman to the rough-and-tumble jock to the sophisticated woman. Even college kids who can barely afford to feed themselves seem to find ways to get their daily fix of the game. Darts is a growing phenomenon that I hope peo- ple everywhere will welcome.

Oh, by the way, Jo-Jo and I, we took first. I'd call it a bullseye. 16

INTERVIEW WITH A MARINE SNIPER

Todd Hoffman

■

Boise State University
Boise, Idaho

Most people don't understand the military force our coun- 1
try possesses," says former United States Marine Corps sniper Steve
Teague, "and the sniper is the most efficient and reliable weapon in the
arsenal. What we can do is incredible." Highly trained and well
equipped, the sniper, as the Marines say, is "a one-man unit with a very
distinct mission"—to hunt and kill the enemy as efficiently as possible
under any circumstances. It is not an occupation that fits the stereotype
of a government job, perhaps not even that of a soldier.

Normally using a high-powered rifle, the sniper's primary func- 2
tion is to engage the enemy and eliminate as many key targets as possible without being detected. This can be accomplished from nearly a
mile away, and, as Teague very seriously states: "Most of the time they
will never know what hit them. If it's a well-placed shot, they won't even
flinch. Lights out!" The sniper cautiously and patiently chooses the target and waits for the right moment while hiding in a "hooch," a hole
dug in the ground covered with the surrounding vegetation. Holding
the crosshairs of his high-powered, telescopic sights steadily on the target's vital areas, such as the upper torso or the base of the skull, the
sniper waits until the right moment, takes a deep breath, lets the breath
halfway out, and slowly squeezes the trigger, trying not to let the report of the rifle surprise him every time. Flinching or shaking in anticipation of the rifle's heavy recoil at the wrong moment could send the

bullet several feet off course. Perhaps the only thought that penetrates the sniper's deep concentration is the motto "one shot, one kill," Steve says. Sometimes, a sniper may be so far away that the bullet, traveling at well over 3,500 feet per second, may take more than a full second to reach its intended destination. After firing no more than twice, the sniper must change positions in order to avoid being detected by the enemy.

"The idea is to never let the enemy know where you are—for obvious reasons," Teague explains academically. "If a sniper does the job properly, the enemy will never know how many people are shooting, which is probably one of the most terrifying situations you could ever be in." Most would agree that this is true for both parties involved, but as Teague states hesitantly, "The military trains you to turn your emotions on and off like a light switch." An advancing enemy's movement will come to a virtual halt as a sniper begins working from ambush. As key targets such as officers and communications personnel are eliminated, chaos sets in and, as Teague says very reluctantly, "That's when we've got them right where we want them." Teague, along with a partner, used these methods in the Gulf War to capture an entire rifle company and two armored vehicles from the elite Iraqi Republican Guard, even though they were outnumbered by a ratio of more than thirty to one.

If the sniper is outnumbered too greatly, however, taking a shot can pose too much of a risk of being captured. Instead of firing, the sniper is forced to act in another capacity, relaying details of the enemy's location, numbers, and equipment back to superiors, giving as much information about the enemy as possible in the process. As Teague reasons, "This is far more deadly for them than shooting at them with a rifle." Once their positions are known, enemy installations can be attacked from above with helicopters, short-range bombers, long-range artillery (from as far away as thirty miles on land or at sea), or with the pinpoint accuracy of a high-altitude bombing strike, all directed by the sniper.

To avoid being detected while performing such tasks, the sniper relies on a number of tactics and pieces of special equipment. "A lot of times after shooting," explains Teague, "we would move directly into the enemy. It's the last thing they expect to happen." Crawling on the ground through the thickest vegetation helps prevent the sniper from being easily detected while moving. Also, by wearing a camouflage suit covered with netting, burlap strips, and bits of surrounding plants and grasses, the sniper becomes virtually invisible to the human eye. A camouflaged sniper can literally creep or sneak up to and lie hiding within a few feet of a foe and never be detected. Radio frequencies are scrambled by high-tech coding devices to prevent the enemy from monitoring communications. A special miniature computer sends hundreds of bits of information in a single burst when connected to the transmitter, which prevents the enemy from locating a sniper's position since these radio transmissions aren't long enough in duration to be tracked. The radio itself is rigged with a high explosive, so that the sniper may destroy it if captured in order to prevent the enemy from obtaining the classified transmitting and receiving frequencies stored in its memory. Using such high-tech resources, the sniper is able to penetrate hundreds of miles into the opposing forces' territory. As Teague states, "That's when we can 'cry havoc and let slip the dogs of war.' "

Entering enemy territory by helicopter, on foot, by parachute from high altitudes, or by sea with scuba equipment from a submarine extends the sniper's range behind enemy lines or even further. The result of such deep penetration is that a sniper can be isolated in hostile terrain for periods of more than a week with minimal equipment and rations. Survival training in a range of environments from deserts to tropical forests is an essential part of a sniper's preparation. Snipers must be skilled at living off the land for days at a time. "They teach you to eat anything that moves," says Teague in a drill instructor's voice. "I've eaten things that would make a billygoat puke: worms, frogs, snakes, roots, berries, leaves, bark. You name it. Fresh water was a luxury half the time." It is this self-sufficiency that makes the sniper so deadly, along with a most basic piece of equipment, the rifle.

6

"Our rifles are precision instruments that cost thousands of dollars apiece," Teague says in a voice indicating his seriousness. "We couldn't do our jobs without them. They are hand built by the best gunsmiths in the world. Even our ammunition is handmade." Specially made for the Marine Corps, the standard bolt action .308-caliber sniper rifle has an accurate-kill range of well over one thousand meters. The semiautomatic .50 caliber that is often used has a range of more than double that and can fire high-explosive, armor-piercing ammunition capable of destroying tanks and other armored vehicles. Both rifles have telescopic sights of twelve-power magnification, or twelve times the power of the human eye, which can be used to read the print on a newspaper at a hundred meters or see the expression on a person's face at five hundred. Night-vision scopes can be attached to both weapons, allowing them to be fired as accurately at night as during the day, a truly devastating potential.

7

"Sergeant Carlos Hathcock had ninety-three confirmed kills dur-   8
ing the Vietnam War," said Teague with a sort of subtle rage in his voice
when I asked about the "effectiveness" of the sniper, "and those were
only the confirmed ones. But killing people isn't something you talk
about. Going to war is something that no one could ever imagine, and
it's something I hope to never do again." While thumbing through a
stack of snapshots from the Gulf War, Teague paused on a picture of
himself, hands on hips in a ragged uniform, standing next to what is
known as a fighting hole, a hole approximately six feet square, surrounded with sandbags, and covered with camouflaged nets. He said,
"This was my home for six months. And it wasn't a very damned nice
place to live either." He paused again briefly, with eyes unfocused, and
then continued, saying, "The Iraqis didn't stand a chance, and neither
would any other country in the world. A sniper is one person who can
do some incredible damage. Our country spends millions of dollars a
year on defense. How many people really know what it is being spent
on, or what really goes on in a war?" He gazed at another photo, this
one of an impossibly high plume of fire spewing upward from an ex-
ploded oil well, surrounded by vehicles charred beyond recognition, the
sky pitch-black at eleven in the morning.

OUR DAILY BREAD

Linda Kampel

•

Pennsylvania State University, York Campus
York, Pennsylvania

To anyone who has the luxury of regular meals and a safe place to call home, walking through the entrance of "Our Daily Bread" soup kitchen is like stepping into a different world. "Our Daily Bread" operates out of a two-room cinder-block building in York, Pennsylvania, that has been transformed into a kitchen and dining area where nearly three hundred poverty-stricken people come every day to eat. The front doors open at 10 A.M., and the first thing you notice when they do is a large room with rows of six-foot metal tables, dim lights that cast gray shadows, and walls that are painted in 1970s "harvest gold" that has dulled with time.

In the back of the room there is a stainless-steel, cafeteria-style serving counter where about thirty-five people are being served hot coffee and donuts. As gloomy as the surroundings may sound, the majority of the people in the place seem to be comfortably familiar with the daily routine of standing in line waiting for lunch to be served. Occasionally, someone tells a joke or a funny story and one or more people will laugh, making the atmosphere seem almost cheery.

As I'm observing the moment, a tall, heavyset black man wearing a dark cap suddenly starts yelling at an invisible companion who has obviously upset him. "F--- you! I'll do what I want!" he yells. Everyone else in the room goes on with their business. "I said I'm going to do what I want. Just leave me alone!"

At first, it seems like this man could be a real threat, but when I 4
ask him what his name is, he very calmly says, "My name's Andy."

There is something sad about the look in Andy's eyes, and, within 5
a few minutes, he's arguing again with whomever it is that has made
him so unhappy. I find it hard to keep from getting involved and wanting to find Andy the help that he obviously seems to need for his problems. It's hard not to feel his pain.

At 11 A.M., the crowd grows to about 80 people, and volunteers are 6
preparing to serve lunch. By 11:30, the number increases to 120, and by
12:15, there are close to 250 men, women, and a handful of children making their way into the line that moves like a well-rehearsed act in a play.
Today's meal consists of vegetable soup, broccoli, bread, and tuna-noodle
casserole, with a choice of either lemonade or coffee to drink. People of
every age, gender, and race move through the line. No one is turned away.

Carol, a thirty-five-year-old black woman dressed in clean but 7
worn-out clothes, says that she has been coming here for about two
years. "Most people who come here aren't homeless," she says. "We all
have a place to live and all. It's just that sometimes meals are a problem. Some people come here because it's a social thing, you know. You
take a break from whatever you're doing. You come in here and have
some food and talk to people you know."

A tall white man, about sixty-five years of age and dressed in dirty 8
old clothes, walks past us. He has donut powder all over his mouth and
chin. "That's so sad." Carol says. "He doesn't even know it's there. That
poor man. Now *he* needs help. At least he's here in a place where he'll
be taken care of."

At first it's easy to think that Carol's problems aren't all that bad, 9
perhaps because she has become so good at convincing herself that this
way of life is normal. You fall right into her train of thought. But later,
thinking back, you can't help realizing that the majority of the people
who come to Our Daily Bread do need help of some kind, or they
wouldn't be there. They're either so lost that they can't find themselves
anymore, or they have accepted this daily routine as the reality of a bad
hand they've been dealt in life.

Around 12:30 P.M., a volunteer worker walks over to a microphone 10
at the end of the serving counter and asks, "Has everyone gotten the
food they need to eat?" No one says a word. "If anyone needs more to
eat, please come up and get as much as you want."

A few people return to the counter for second helpings, but most 11
people are beginning to leave. They've been well fed, and maybe somehow given the boost they need to make it through the day.

At the helm of this well-run operation are two people, Joe Mc-   12
Cormick and Marie Rohleder, both of whom have a genuine and un-
conditional interest in making sure that for at least two and a half hours
a day, anyone who needs a hot meal or emotional support in a warm,
dry place can find it within these walls.

Joe McCormick, the business manager, is a tall, white-haired,   13
sixty-year-old man whose smile lets you know right away that he is a
very special human being, the "real thing." Joe cares about every inch
of this place, and about the people who come here for help. Joe is semi-
retired now, but he still takes care of all the expenses of Our Daily Bread,
keeps track of the donations, and sends out thank-you notes to all those
who contribute food or services. Every Monday, Joe is in charge of food
preparation and then oversees the serving operation.

"We've been here for seven years now," he says. "We're open   14
Monday through Friday from 10 A.M. to 12:30 P.M. You should have
seen the place we were in before we moved here. It was hell on earth,
in the basement of Cristo Salvador, a local Spanish church. The kitchen
was about a third of the size of this one here. There was barely enough
room for a dishwasher and a stove. That place used to get about 150
degrees in the summertime when we were making food, and there were
times when the water on the floor from rainstorms was six inches deep.
We were afraid to use anything electric." Joe lights a cigarette. "Back
then we were serving about 107 people a day. Now we're serving around
300. It used to be 400 before September House started its senior citizen outreach program, but I'll let Marie tell you about that later."

Cartons of pastries arrive through the back door, so Joe goes over   15
to help bring them in. When he returns, he leans against a stack of
crates.

"Last Thanksgiving we were really sweating it out because we sup-   16
ply Helping Hands with their turkeys, and we hardly had any turkeys
at all. Then right after the holidays, we got a call to come and pick up
fifty of them. It's feast or famine around here. When Chuck E. Cheese
closed down last year, I got two truckloads of pizzas and birthday cakes.
Boy, were they good. People still come in here and ask, 'Do you have
any more of those birthday cakes?' We're never at a loss for resources
for food, it seems. It's not always the greatest, but it's out there. York
County is a very giving place."

Joe tells me, "Just a second," and when he returns, he is with a   17
dark-haired woman about thirty-five years of age and wearing a blue
nylon jacket. She has the same welcoming smile that Joe has, and I can't
help thinking how lucky everyone here is to have these two people on

their side. Joe introduces the woman as Marie who is, by her own definition, the inventory control specialist.

"In other words, I make sure that all the food gets put in the   18
freezer, which explains the jacket. I also rotate the food on the shelves
so that nothing stays around too long."

Marie also takes on the responsibilities of food preparation and   19
serving operations on Thursdays and Fridays.

"There's a guy named Charlie who takes care of Tuesdays and   20
Wednesdays, but he's not here right now. Anyway, an organization
called September House started an outreach program a couple of years
ago. They go and pick up our senior citizens and take them for meals
at their senior citizen center. They're much better off over there, because they get the attention they really need. That's why the number
of people we serve here has dropped off slightly. It's a wonderful organization. It's hard not to get involved sometimes. There are some people you can't help but get involved with. They need that. And there are
some people who come and go. We just found out today that one fellow we get involved with *a lot* just got sent to jail last night. Busted for
drugs. It's heartbreaking sometimes because you know how hard they've
been trying. There was one guy who used to do dishes for us. Lester.
He tried *so* hard to stay sober, and he just couldn't do it. Eventually he
died from alcohol poisoning."

"That's the hardest kind," Joe says. "You see these people and you   21
know that no matter what the hell they do, they're in a hole. And they're
never gonna get out."

One of the volunteers comes over and asks where to put a tray   22
filled with pumpkin bread.

"That's Pat," Marie says after she points her toward a storage   23
shelf. "She's one of our regular volunteers. She comes in almost every
day, along with the volunteers from at least one church group. We get
about fifty volunteers a week. The only problem is that no one wants
to clean up—everyone wants to serve or cook, but as soon as 12:30 hits,
boom, they're out the door. York College is sending over a group of students this Saturday to paint these walls. And the group Up with People is coming in tomorrow, I think, to help out. I'm glad they're coming because Fridays are the worst. For some reason that's the day when
the people who really are in desperate need come in, so that they can
load up for the weekend. We always have extra bread, so we can give
out a couple of loaves to everyone."

When 12:45 arrives, the volunteers are finished serving lunch.   24
There is clean-up work to be done, and Joe and Marie take their place

among the volunteers so that they will soon be able to call it a day. As I start to leave, it is hard to know how to feel. On one hand, it's really sad to see people trying to survive without the daily things that most of us take for granted. On the other hand, until it isn't necessary for people to have to worry about where their next meal will come from, it's comforting to know that wonderful people like Joe and Marie at Our Daily Bread are out there doing their best to ease some of the burden.

BEHIND THE SUGAR CURTAIN

Melanie Papenfuss

·

University of North Dakota
Grand Forks, North Dakota

Ten-thirty on a Friday night I pull into my cousin Blaine's 1
farmyard. The old white two-story house is dark. I grab my overnight
bag from the backseat and quickly make my way into the house. Silence.
I know Blaine is home: his pick-up is in the driveway. I flick on the
kitchen light and look around. What a mess!

During beet season, which runs from the first week in October 2
until all the beets are out of the ground, I expect the house to be messy,
but nothing like this. A red and white cooler is sitting on the table, half
open. Through the crack I can see empty sandwich bags, two cans of
Coke, and an empty bag of Ruffles potato chips. On the counter sits a
box of Wheaties and a carton of milk, still waiting to be put away.
Dishes are piled high in the sink. My eyes wander to the living room.
The hide-a-bed is laying out, obviously being used regularly. Dirty
laundry is scattered about.

"Melanie, is that you?" 3

From the bedroom, Blaine walks out, wearing a pair of old bas- 4
ketball shorts. Dark brown hair, matted on one side of his head and
sticking out on the other, sleepy eyes, and a groggy voice materialize
before my eyes.

"You're just getting up?" I stare in disbelief. 5

"Ya," he replies while rubbing the sleep from his eyes. "I work at 6
night and sleep by day. I am lucky enough to have been given the night

shift rather than the day." As an afterthought he looks at what he is wearing, or not wearing. "Let me get dressed."

He returns with a red turtleneck, red and black flannel shirt, and faded Wrangler jeans.   7

"My shift starts at midnight, but I like to be in the field by 11:30." The left side of his upper lip curls into a cocky smirk. "Do you think you can handle an all-nighter?"   8

Before I can answer he continues. "What do you want to bring to eat—sandwiches, chips, cookies, Rice Krispies bars, Coke, Pepsi, Dr. Pepper?"   9

"I thought this was for twelve hours, not twelve days!" I simply shrug, "Pack what you like."   10

Quickly he throws together four salami and cheese sandwiches, a bag of chips, some Rice Krispies bars, and a six-pack of Coke. After the food supply is safely tucked away, we go into the living room to catch a weather report.   11

The announcer blasts, "For all you farmers, you can expect clear skies. Those stars will shine tonight!"   12

Blaine jumps out of his chair and flicks the TV off. "That's all I needed to hear. Let's go."   13

He grabs the cooler and his red St. Thomas Standard jacket and walks out the door. I shut off the lights and quickly follow.   14

We reach the field at 11:15 P.M. All I can see from the road is a large light emanating from the middle of the field. I look closer, and alongside the bright light I can see orange parking lights suspended in mid-air. Blaine turns into the field and heads toward the light.   15

A gruff voice comes from the CB. "Blaine, is that you?"   16

"Ya, John, and I have a passenger tonight. You remember Melanie, don't ya?" Blaine looks at me and winks.   17

"I sure do," John replies with a chuckle. A large older man with silver hair and wire-rimmed glasses, John is the owner of all the beets. "Kevin should be back with the truck in about fifteen minutes. You can take over then."   18

We pass the machine producing the light. It is a 4440 John Deere tractor with four headlights. Behind it a weird-looking contraption is being pulled. It looks like a plow or cultivator but with a long armlike structure that rises up and disappears into the box.   19

"What is that thing behind the tractor?"   20

Blaine laughs, "That 'thing' is the beet lifter. It pulls the beets up and into the truck box."   21

"Oh."   22

We reach the other side of the field, and Blaine stops the pick-   23
up. I turn and watch the beet lifter inch its way across the field. It reminds me of a snail creeping up and down the glass of a fish tank.

It's not long before I see headlights coming from the north. It is   24
Kevin's truck. He turns into the field, comes halfway in, and stops. I
am confused. Patiently I wait for him to continue toward us, but he
doesn't. Instead I see his box begin to lift slowly into the air.

"What is he doing?"   25

"Do you mean Kevin?" Eagerly I nod yes. "He's dumping the left-   26
over dirt." Blaine shifts his body toward me and focuses his attention
on my question. "You see, after you unload your beets at the plant, the
dirt and beets are separated by the grab rollers and you get your dirt
back. So then you put it back in the field it came from."

As Kevin drives toward us, Blaine grabs the cooler and tilts his   27
head in the direction of the truck. "That's where we're spending the
night, so take everything you need."

The beet truck is a yellow-and-brown Mack truck. To get into   28
the cab, I have to step onto a runner that is a foot and a half off the
ground. There is even a handle on the left side that is perpendicular to
the ground. The inside of the cab is small. There are two seats that
squeak as you sit down. Between the seats is a cubbyhole for storage.
On the steering wheel is a stainless steel knob to help the driver turn.

Blaine turns the radio on to KFGO, a country station. "Jason's   29
truck is full; that means we take over."

Jason, I think, must be the other driver. Blaine pushes in the   30
clutch and grinds the gears into first. The truck jerks to a slow start.
Carefully Blaine pulls the truck box underneath the lifter and CBs to
John to tell him we're ready.

Before long I hear the thudding of the beets in the empty box.   31
"How do you know when to pull forward or move back to allow the
beets to fill the truck evenly?"

"Do you see those arrows?" Blaine says, pointing out his window   32
to a panel of orange arrows attached to the tractor. "When I need to
speed up or slow down, John flicks a switch and the appropriate arrow
lights up."

"Oh."   33

After a few rounds (a round is one row of beets that runs the en-   34
tire length of the field), the truck is loaded. Now we head north on the
small country road for a mile until we reach a paved road. There we
turn east. It's twelve miles to the Crystal Sugar Beet Plant in Drayton,
North Dakota.

"How fast do you go?" 35

"With a full load I don't like to go over fifty. Empty I will go sixty 36
to sixty-five."

On the road to the plant we meet many empty trucks. Blaine can 37
tell me who is driving and where they are heading by seeing only the
headlights and the color of the truck.

After twenty minutes, we reach the road that will take us to the 38
plant. We get in line with a few other trucks. Their boxes are heaping
with beets.

"Is our truck heaping too?" 39

Amused, Blaine replies, "Yes." 40

"Why don't the beets fly off when you are going down the high- 41
way?"

"Because each beet weighs five to ten pounds. They're too heavy 42
to fly off."

It takes only a few minutes to reach the scale house. When we get 43
up to the scale house window, Blaine rummages through some index
cardlike metal plates and hands one to the woman in the window. I hear
a stamp, and she gives Blaine a slip of paper.

"What did you just do? What's that metal thing?" 44

"This metal thing is a number plate," Blaine explains patiently. 45
"It is recorded by the scale house. The number tells them who owns
the beets in the truck and how heavy the truck is when it's loaded."

I turn and look to see where we are going. We are driving on a 46
single-lane paved road, but at the end it branches out into eight separate roads, spread out like the bristles of a broom. At the end of each is
an orange machine (the piler); trucks are driving up onto them.

Again we wait behind other trucks. When it's our turn, a man in 47
a hardhat signals for us to pull ahead. Slowly Blaine releases the clutch
and drives the big truck onto the piler. There are railings on each side
of us and I don't think we'll fit, but I am wrong. Behind the truck the
ramp is being raised so it is perpendicular to the ground. Then Blaine
gets a signal that tells him to back up so the truck box gate is against
the inclined ramp. When this is done, Blaine can then begin to raise
the truck bed and dump the beets. Once the beets are dumped, the piler
separates the excess dirt from the beets. From there the beets go up a
long conveyor belt and are piled on many other beets. The dirt is
brought to a type of holding bin and is then dumped back into the truck
after it comes off the piler.

We make our way back up the broom bristle and head for the scale 48
house. Blaine hands the woman in the window the paper with his loaded

weight, and she stamps it with his empty weight. We have been carrying 44,000 pounds of beets—twenty-two tons!

"So, now you've seen what goes on during beet season. What do you think?" 49

"I never knew all the things that go on," I said in amazement. "How many more loads will we get to do before your shift is over?" 50

"Probably five or six more if we have no breakdowns. Do you want to go home or keep going?" 51

"Are you kidding?" I reply eagerly. "Pass me a Coke, would ya?" 52

CHAPTER 5

EXPLAINING CONCEPTS

S*ome writers claim there's only one rule:* be interesting. *Perhaps this is true. But how does a writer* become *interesting? Is there some pattern, formula, or principle to follow, some trick to apply? One way to discover the answer is to watch other writers at work, analyzing their techniques to understand* how *they create interest as they simultaneously present information. The essays in this chapter are interesting* and *highly informative, and very much worth examining for their technique.*

All of them pull you in and make you want *to read on. Choice of subject matter is part of it. Cannibalism, animated Disney films, procrastination, and domestic violence are concepts that pique readers' curiosity. But subject matter alone does not an essay make. Pay attention to the strategies these writers use to draw you in, focus their subjects, present information, and make themselves credible. Notice, in particular, how thoroughly all four use and document sources.*

If interest is one criterion for judging successful explanatory writing, then Linh Kieu Ngo scores a direct hit with the subject of cannibalism. Call it unnatural obsession or simply morbid curiosity, the word cannibalism *is like glue that fixes readers to the page. This isn't to take away from Ngo's skill at* keeping *readers interested, which is considerable. After he establishes the existence of modern-day cannibalism with a stunning narrative opening, he classifies the types of cannibalism and discusses each in thoroughly informative, well-documented fashion. His tone throughout is factual, almost scientific, and always engaging.*

Janet Walker identifies a pattern in the female characters in Walt Disney's animated films and uses the pattern to explain a concept that she calls the "Disney Girl." Her technique is to use vivid sketches that reveal a striking commonality among Snow White, Cinderella, Sleeping Beauty, Ariel, and Belle, creating an explanation that is freshly informative for readers who are familiar with the subject, but who haven't thought about it in the way Walker has. It is worth noting, as well, how she controls the flow of information to keep the pace of her essay lively and engaging. Read carefully to see how Walker creates her voice in the pages of this essay.

In her essay, "The Art of Wasting Time," Anna Pride opens with a voice that effectively hooks readers by establishing common ground. Everyone, after all, has wasted time one way or another. Pride maintains the authority of her voice by systematically exploring the concept of procrastination and the range of physiological, psychological, and sociological explanations that try to account for it. As in Linh Kieu Ngo's essay on cannibalism, the inherent "interest" factor in Pride's topic works to pull readers forward. Notice how she invokes and effectively uses a cultural tendency present in readers, that is, the tendency for people to like to read themselves into the subject. Don't feel alone if you find yourself reading Pride's essay with great interest because you're thinking, "Gee, sometimes I'm a little (or a lot) like that myself. I wonder why?" If the writer's rule is "make it interesting," then Pride succeeds. The desire to understand and perhaps explain ourselves keeps us reading with great interest.

Hobi Reader takes an entirely different tack in "Battered-Woman Syndrome." Rather than an opening move to establish common ground with readers, she introduces her subject by putting it in a category that will distance readers from it: spousal abuse and wife beating as acceptable behavior is hardly something that readers will embrace. By establishing distance rather than proximity between readers and her subject, the writer is able to work a different strategy toward her objective of explaining battered-woman syndrome. You might also note the balanced tone that permeates Reader's essay, and the way that facts and logic are used to convey the emotional and psychological horror of the subject.

After detailing the most prominent characteristics of battered-woman syndrome, the essay addresses two questions that keep readers fixed to the page: why does battering occur, and why do women remain in abusive relationships? While the answers are less than pleasant, the context that Reader creates for them makes the answers plausible, logical, and credible. The emotional appeal that is created, in effect, by careful logic throughout the essay seems fully to justify the plea that is entered in the final paragraph: we must stop the ugly cycle of such abuse.

Cannibalism: It Still Exists

Linh Kieu Ngo

•

University of California, San Diego
La Jolla, California

Fifty-five Vietnamese refugees fled to Malaysia on a small fish-   1
ing boat to escape communist rule in their country following the Vietnam War. During their escape attempt, the captain was shot by the coast
guard. The boat and its passengers managed to outrun the coast guard
to the open sea, but they had lost the only person that knew the way to
Malaysia, the captain.

The men onboard tried to navigate the boat, but after a week fuel   2
ran out and they drifted further out to sea. Their supply of food and
water was gone; people were starving, and some of the elderly were near
death. The men managed to produce a small amount of drinking water
by boiling salt water, using dispensable wood from the boat to create a
small fire near the stern. They also tried to fish, but had little success.

A month went by, and the old and weak died. At first, the crew   3
threw the dead overboard; but later, out of desperation, the crew turned
to human flesh as a source of food. Some people vomited as they at-
tempted to eat it, while others refused to resort to cannibalism and see
the bodies of their loved ones sacrificed for food. Those who did not
eat died of starvation, and their bodies in turn became food for others.
Human flesh was cut out, washed in salt water, and hung to dry for
preservation. The liquids inside the cranium were eaten to quench
thirst. The livers, kidneys, heart, stomach, and intestines were boiled
and eaten.

Five months passed before a whaling vessel discovered the drifting boat, looking like a graveyard of bones. There was only one survivor. 4

Cannibalism, the act of human beings eating human flesh (Sagan 2), can be broken down into two main categories: exocannibalism, the eating of outsiders or foreigners, and endocannibalism, the eating of members of one's own social group (Shipman 70). Within these categories are several functional types of cannibalism, three of the most common being survival cannibalism, dietary cannibalism, and religious and ritual cannibalism. 5

Survival cannibalism occurs when people trapped without food have to decide "whether to starve or eat fellow humans" (Shipman 70). In the case of the Vietnamese refugees, the crew and passengers on the boat ate human flesh to stay alive. They did not kill a person to get human flesh for nourishment, but instead waited until people had died. Even after human carcasses were sacrificed as food, the boat people ate only enough to survive. Another case of survival cannibalism occurred when General Douglas MacArthur's forces cut supply lines to Japanese troops stationed in the Pacific islands in 1945. In one incident, Japanese troops were reported to have sacrificed the Arapesh people of northeastern New Guinea for food (Tuzin 63) in order to avoid death by starvation. 6

Unlike survival cannibalism, where humans are eaten as a last resort, in dietary cannibalism, humans are eaten as a part of a culture. In survival cannibalism, humans are eaten after they have passed away, but in dietary cannibalism, humans are purchased or trapped for food. Survival cannibalism often involves people eating other people of the same origins, while dietary cannibalism usually involves people eating foreigners. 7

In the society of the Miyanmin of the West Sepik interior of Papua, New Guinea, the villagers do not value human flesh over that of pigs or marsupials because human flesh is part of their diet (Poole 7). To the Miyanmin people, there are no differences between "gender, kinship, ritual status, and bodily substance," and they eat anyone, even their own dead, practicing both endocannibalism and exocannibalism; to ensure that they have a supply of human flesh for food, they raid neighboring tribes, dragging their victims back to their village to be eaten (Poole 11). Perhaps, in the history of this society, there was at one time a shortage of wild game to be hunted for food, and because people were more plentiful than fish, deer, rabbits, pigs, or cows, survival cannibalism was adopted as a last resort. Then, as their culture de- 8 veloped, the Miyanmin retained the practice of cannibalism, so that dietary cannibalism has endured as a part of their tradition.

Similar to the Miyanmin, the people of the Leopard and Alligator societies in South America eat human flesh as part of their cultural tradition. Practicing dietary exocannibalism, the Leopard people hunt in groups, with one member wearing the skin of a leopard to conceal his face. They ambush their victims in the forest and carry their victims back to their village to be eaten. The Alligator people also hunt in groups, but they hide themselves under a canoelike submarine that resembles an alligator, then swim close to a fisherman's or trader's canoe to overturn it and catch their victims (MacCormack 54).

It is believed that warfare and cannibalism are connected (Sagan 3), which may explain why the Alligator and the Leopard people are cannibals. Two warring villages may well seek to try to kill one another off, eating their enemies to celebrate their victory. Over many years, killing and eating humans becomes a part of the culture, and any foreigners trespassing on their lands who are thought of as enemies are killed and eaten.

Religious or ritual cannibalism is different from survival and dietary cannibalism, in that it has a ceremonial purpose rather than one of nourishment. Sometimes, only a single victim is sacrificed in a ritual, while at other times, many are sacrificed. Among the Bangala tribe along the Congo River in central Africa, when a powerful chief or a former leader dies, the members of the tribe purchase, sacrifice, and feast on slaves to honor him (Sagan 53). The number of slaves sacrificed is determined by how highly the tribe revered the deceased leader.

Ritual cannibalism among South American Indians often serves as revenge for the dead. Like the Bangalas along the Congo, some South American tribes kill their victims to be served as part of funeral rituals, with human sacrifices denoting that the deceased was held in high honor. Also like the Bangalas, these tribes use outsiders as victims. Unlike the Bangalas, however, the Indians sacrifice only one victim instead of many in their rites. For example, when a warrior of a tribe is killed in battle, the family of the warrior forces a victim to take the identity of the warrior. They adorn the victim with the deceased warrior's belongings, and the deceased warrior's wives may even marry him. But after the family feels the victim has assumed the spiritual identity of the warrior, the family kills him. The children in the tribe soak their hands in the victim's blood as a symbol that they have revenged the death of the warrior. Old women from the tribe drink the blood of the victim, and then they cut up his body to be roasted and eaten (Sagan 53–54).

By sacrificing a victim, the people of the tribe ensure that the death of the warrior is avenged so that the soul of the deceased can rest in peace.

In the villages of certain African tribes, only a small part of a dead   13
body is used in ritual cannibalism. In these tribes, the child-bearing capacity of women is highly valued, and women are obligated to eat small raw fragments of genital parts during fertility rites. Elders of the tribe supervise its women to ensure that they will be fertile. In the Bimin-Kuskusmin tribe, a widow eats a small, raw fragment of flesh from the penis of her deceased husband in order to enhance her future fertility and reproductive capacity. Similarly, a widower may eat a raw fragment of flesh from his deceased wife's vagina along with a fragment of her bone marrow; by eating her flesh, he hopes to strengthen the fertility capacity of his daughters borne by his dead wife, and by eating her bone marrow, he honors her reproductive capacity. Also, when an elder woman of the village who has shown great reproductive capacity dies, her uterus and the interior parts of her vagina are eaten by other women who hope to further benefit from her reproductive power (Poole 16–17).

Members of developed societies in general practice none of these   14
forms of cannibalism, with the exception, perhaps, of survival cannibalism when the only alternative is starvation. It is possible, however, that our distant-past ancestors were cannibals who through the eons turned away from the practice. We are, after all, descended from the same ancestors as the Miyanmin, the Alligator, and the Leopard people, and survival cannibalism shows that many are capable of eating human flesh when they have no other choice.

Works Cited

Brown, Paula, and Donald Tuzin, eds. *The Ethnography of Cannibalism*. Washington: Society for Psychological Anthropology, 1983.

MacCormack, Carol. "Human Leopard and Crocodile." Brown and Tuzin 54–55.

Poole, Fitz John Porter. "Cannibals, Tricksters, and Witches." Brown and Tuzin 6–17.

Sagan, Eli. *Cannibalism*. New York: Harper, 1976.

Shipman, Pat. "The Myths and Perturbing Realities of Cannibalism." *Discover* Mar. 1987: 70+.

Tuzin, Donald. "Cannibalism and Arapesh Cosmology." Brown and Tuzin 61–63.

THE DISNEY GIRL

Janet Walker

■

Augusta College
Augusta, Georgia

Ah, to be a Disney Girl! To possess beauty so divine it can 1
melt the hearts of charming princes and gruff miners alike. To be able
to use the gift of angelic song to tame temperamental beasts and attract
otherwise timid forest creatures. To know that, in the end—despite the
fact that your wicked stepmother has forced you into a life of servitude
and an evil queen is seeking your mutilated heart—yes, in the end, some
day your prince will come.

The Disney conception of the perfect girl can be described, with 2
little exception, in this way: she is always pretty, always fair, always
model thin, always endowed with a beautiful singing voice, and always
at the mercy of some malevolent, often jealous, older woman. The Disney Girl also has the love of a handsome, wealthy, and brave man, almost always of royal blood. Though rooted in medieval and Victorian
folklore and literature, these female characters are most familiar to us
dipped in Disney's colorful animation and sprinkled with his magical
fairy dust so that we have forgotten their origins and given them an
identity that can only be described as, well, *Disney*.

Let's start with the original Disney Girl, Snow White. Snow 3
White epitomizes what "gorgeous" represented in the 1930s; in other
words, Disney allowed her to be a little fat by today's standards. Still,
most of us would agree with the evil queen's magic mirror, that this Dis-

ney Girl, with her skin as white as snow, lips as red as blood, and hair as black as ebony, is, indeed, "the fairest one of all."   4

Setting the pattern for Disney Girls to come, Snow White's beauty is of such perfection and innocence and downright sugar-and-spice-ness that even animals (in her case, forest creatures) love her—and even help her with the housework! With these same qualities, she charms her way out of death: the huntsman hired by the jealous queen to kill her and bring back her heart as proof of the deed is so touched by Snow White's beauty that he lets her go. She then wins over seven rustic dwarf miners (even one whose grumpiness is his trademark) and—wouldn't you know it?—a handsome prince, who just happens to be riding through the forest at the same time that she just happens to be singing one of the loveliest, most delusory ballads ever written, the one that proclaims in tremulous soprano, "Some . . . day . . . my prince . . . will come. . . ." Jack Zipes points out the narrow middle-class assumptions that inform this wish-fantasy when he discusses it as "a conception of women, work, and child-rearing . . . [common to] bourgeois circles more . . . than to . . . the peasantry and aristocracy" (53). In other words, where does this highly idealized concept of the "prince" as savior come from? Zipes calls Walt Disney "that twentieth century sanitation man" (53) for his skill at denying any value systems that fall outside of American middle class.   5

Another dimension of the Disney Girl concept is reflected in Cinderella: blond, thin, beautiful, and fair—but not "snow" white; she has something of a tan. Her beauty is such that even hidden under rags it evokes great jealousy in her stepmother and ugly stepsisters, and they assign her a life of thankless servitude. While washing the castle floors on hands and knees, Cinderella bursts into an angelic rendition of "Sing, Sweet Nightingale," and with her lovely voice charms the house dog, yard animals, and castle mice. She also exhibits the positive inner qualities of humility, industriousness, and patience, but none of these is what captivates the handsome prince whom she meets at a royal find-a-wife-for-the-prince ball. Instead, he decides to marry her on the basis of her physical beauty and tiny feet! If Cinderella and her prince have worries of divorce or aging, you can't tell it by the way they ride into "Happily ever after" at the end. These events fit a larger historical pattern pointed out by Antonia Fraser in *The Weaker Vessel:* "Let us begin with a wedding. That was after all how most women in the early seventeenth century were held to begin their lives" (9). It is not a sense of willful independence but one of romantic dependence that characterizes the

Disney Girl. Perhaps this conception only taps a norm that has deeply permeated Anglo and American culture. Louise Tilley talks about this depth when she says, "With the possible exception of the Anglo-Saxon period, the norm . . . was that a woman would marry, bear children and live out her life with a husband who had legally sanctioned rights over her and their children" (x). In the Disney version, it's just that we never see beyond the glorious romantic norm of the wedding day.

Next in the Disney pantheon is Princess Aurora. Better known as 6 Sleeping Beauty, she is a slender, blond teenager whose loveliness, again, enchants sylvan creatures and whose physical beauty and heavenly singing capture a prince who happens to be, what else, riding through the forest. At first, Sleeping Beauty's life is virtually carefree because she is watched over by bumbling, well-meaning fairies who protect her from the knowledge of a dreadful truth: at the little princess's birth, a spurned sorceress, Maleficent, placed a curse on her that proclaimed she would prick her finger on the needle of a spinning wheel and die before her sixteenth birthday. This happens, and, of course, the forest creatures and inhabitants of the king's domain are in despair.

But not to worry! In steps a handsome prince who twice delivers 7 Sleeping Beauty from death—first by kissing her back to life, then by slaying the evil Maleficent, who has taken on the form of a fire-breathing dragon. In the end, the prince weds Sleeping Beauty and the two live, we assume, happily ever after. According to Max Luthi, it is characteristic of the fairy tale to "fill its hearers with the confidence that a new, larger life is to come after the deathlike sleep—that, after the isolation, a new form of contact and community will follow" (24). Perhaps even more interesting is the extent to which the male prince rescuing the female princess from death symbolizes, according to Julius Heuscher, "the highest expression of a young man's love for a woman" (88).

Although most of the basic elements remain the same, the Dis- 8 ney Girl has changed in some ways over the years. For instance, Disney recently broke box office records with a Disney Girl who is not a girl at all, but a fish! Yet, however ichthyo, Ariel, the beloved Little Mermaid, is still fair and lovely, auburn haired and shapely. And like any good Disney Girl, she has a prince, handsome and daring Eric, who falls in love with her enchanting voice (as do a variety of undersea creatures). Ariel's antagonist, the wicked sea witch Ursula, envies the kingship of Ariel's father and uses the beautiful mermaid as a lure to get to the throne. In the end, however, Eric slays the sea witch and marries Ariel, sweeping her *onto* her feet to begin life as a human being.

Belle, of *Beauty and the Beast*, with light brown hair, fair skin,   9
pretty face, and graceful features, fits the physical profile of the Disney
Girl, but change is evident in that her prince comes in another form:
he is a man transformed into a beast. Also, unlike Disney Girls of the
past, Belle *effects* change instead of waiting around for it to happen: she
sacrifices her own freedom to release her father from durance, and it is
the power of her inner beauty, not just her outward appearance, that
eventually brings to the fore the Beast's good nature. However, true to
the Disney Girl tradition, Belle is ultimately rewarded for her good-
ness. She becomes the wife of a handsome and *very* muscular prince
(marking a small change from the soft-looking heroes who wedded her
predecessors).

Another evolution in the model of the Disney Girl can be seen in   10
the heroine of Disney's latest venture, *Aladdin*. Princess Jasmine is neither blond nor fair, but a woman of color: Middle Eastern. Instead of
waiting for a prince to deliver her to a life of luxury, she already lives
in such a state and falls in love with a fascinating, good-hearted peas-
ant boy. Like a true Disney lass, however, she remains pretty, her voice
remains distinctly Caucasian, and, in the end, she still gets her man and
lives happily ever after.

As a child, I myself was not very pretty; in fact, I was funny look-   11
ing. But I comforted myself with the notion that something magical
would happen to me during adolescence. I would become, without any
effort on my part but by nature's irresistible hand, a Sleeping Beauty,
a Cinderella, or—if you can believe this, considering the fact that I am
black—a Snow White. No such thing happened, of course. But then,
that's life outside the realm of the Disney Girl. No relief shows up on
a white horse or with a magic wand. When the going gets tough, or you
find yourself without a date on Saturday night, you just deal with it.

It may be a comfort to know that while we're sweating it out over   12
what reality offers—from menstrual cramps and bad-hair days to
"princes" who turn out to be portly, blue collar, and dragon shy—
there's always a Disney Girl to live out our fantasies for us. But it's also
important to make sure—for ourselves and especially for our children—that we understand the power of these images. According to Jack
Zipes, fairy tales "offer a pseudo-criticism of real social conditions to
guarantee that children of all classes will mind their manners and preserve the *status quo*—all to the advantage of those who control the dominant discourse" (99). Although the animation is superb and the stories
full of enchantment, wizardry, and the basic satisfaction of good tri-
umphing over evil, we should not let ourselves be misled into believ-

ing that Cinderella, Snow White, Belle, and the rest represent the epitome of the ideal woman. Those who do might find themselves in the same predicament Cinderella did after the midnight chimes: sprawled on their backsides in the dust, with their dreams dashed to pieces around them.

Works Cited

Fraser, Antonia. *The Weaker Vessel.* New York: Knopf, 1984.

Heuscher, Julius E. *A Psychiatric Study of Fairy Tales: Their Origin, Meaning and Usefulness.* Springfield, MA: Thomas, 1963.

Luthi, Max. *Once upon a Time: On the Nature of Fairy Tales.* New York: Ungar, 1970.

Tilley, Louise A. Introduction. *The English Woman in History.* Doris May Stenton. New York: Shocken, 1977.

Zipes, Jack. *Fairy Tales and the Art of Subversion — The Classical Genre for Children and the Process of Civilization.* New York: Methuen, 1988.

THE ART OF WASTING TIME

Anna Pride

•

Augusta College
Augusta, Georgia

I t is three in the morning, and a haggard man puts the finish- 1
ing touches on a presentation that he has had a month to complete. A
bright young boy scurries around the backyard collecting bugs for his
big science project due the next morning. A grown woman packs at two
in the morning for her six-thirty business trip. A man disappoints his
wife with a gift of socks for Christmas, which was all he could find on
Christmas Eve. What is wrong with these people? Have they been
stricken with mononucleosis or chronic fatigue syndrome? A death in
the family? Why do normal, intelligent people fritter their time away
and wait till the last possible moment to do the necessary? In a word,
procrastination.

This phenomenon defies logic. Every other ugly duty is "gotten 2
over with." We gulp down our proverbial green beans, always saving
the best for last. Retirement comes after work, M&Ms after nasty medicine, and a soak in the tub after you scour it. It follows that every other
distasteful job would be treated the same way. Aunt Nelda's birthday
present, the big research paper, a visit to the dentist, and the cat's bath
should be *gotten over with* like our green beans and medicine. For many
people, however, they aren't.

Procrastination is not just a bad habit; it is a condition of mind 3
that has some serious causes and consequences. Far too often, substan-
dard work is the result of putting things off until the last moment.

85

When we procrastinate, we don't actually enjoy the time we waste. Instead, we add to our stress level by letting a project worry us for an extended period of time. To understand this paradoxical and self-defeating approach to challenging situations, we must assess what the process of procrastination involves. This common practice of wasting time has both physiological and mental causes and effects.

The art of procrastinating has been developed by humans as a method of coping. It is said that when faced with an overwhelming situation, we either have to laugh or cry. Many of us, on the other hand, just procrastinate. Daunting tasks tax all our faculties and need to be put aside if we are to complete our other duties. Some problems can be too challenging or too far out of our range of experience. If we started early and devoted ourselves to writing that speech, studying for that exam, or firing that friend, we would have time for little else. The bills wouldn't get paid, the kids wouldn't get fed, and the goldfish would go belly up. When asked to choose between carrying out our necessary everyday roles and performing an overwhelming task, the choice is easy: we do the small stuff. 4

When consequences are *lose-lose*, we are forced to choose the lesser of two evils. The choice between two situations that both have potentially negative consequences is called an avoidance-avoidance choice by psychologists. According to Rod Plotnic, "as the time to decide in an avoidance-avoidance situation grows near, we often change our minds many times. Usually we wait until the last minute before making the final decision and [then] deal with the disagreeable consequences" (503). An avoidance-avoidance conflict is like having two crying babies to change and only one diaper. After the unpleasant task is completed, we still have one crying baby with a dirty diaper. On these occasions, procrastination is an ironic attempt to save our sanity. 5

We have all been told that everything has a time and a place. Procrastination is a subconscious way of letting us know that we are attempting a project at the wrong time. All challenges need to ferment in our minds. Procrastination is an attempt to buy more of this necessary reflection time. The conscious intellect understands all too well that the paper is due tomorrow, but all that the brute database will understand is that more time is necessary to collate, organize, and assimilate the three Russian novels that were just read. We often need to mull over the details of a situation before we act. In order to make an intelligent decision when buying a car, for example, we have to consider the range of models, prices, and payment plans. 6

Procrastination can also be a matter of stalling. The brain needs 7 more time to do its work, so the will begins to filibuster. Just as when we need sleep, we yawn, and when we need water, our throats get dry: when we haven't taken ample time to debate a topic, we feel an overpowering urge to procrastinate.

For every task and for every person there is an optimum level of arousal. This level is controlled by our nervous system in a function called homeostasis, which is "the tendency of the autonomic nervous system to maintain the body's internal environment in a balanced state of optimum functioning" (Plotnic 63). The nervous system regulates hormone and chemical levels in the body and, when faced with a challenge, attempts to bring us to an appropriate level of functioning. This is why our hearts race when we see blue lights and hear a siren, and why a hero has such steely calm in a life-or-death situation. If this perfect level of functioning is not reached, we often don't feel motivated even to attempt a task. Clearing hurdles at a track meet requires a high level of arousal. Writing a good paper, or drafting a proposal, requires a sharpness not usually present in the routine of everyday life. People who work well under pressure have a high optimum level of arousal. Our autonomic nervous system brings us to the perfect level of mental awareness necessary to accomplish each task. For this reason, we often procrastinate until the appropriate hormonal and chemical levels are reached—that is, until the heat is on. 8

One can go overboard with this concept, of course. The problems associated with procrastination arise when we wait too long, attempt a project too large, and are too overly aroused or burnt out to function optimally. Such a circumstance is in direct contradiction to the Yerkes-Doddson law, which states that easy tasks require high levels of arousal and difficult tasks require medium to low levels of arousal (Rathus 254). In other words, you can't take a math test when you are stimulated to the point of tears. 9

Many a night I have wondered why I am still wide awake on the eastern side of midnight. I have had plenty of time to complete the project at hand, yet there I sit. Is it because I have single-handedly consumed two pots of coffee? Is it just because I need more time to process the information? Or was the assignment just too overwhelming to complete in daylight hours? Perhaps I can tell my professor that I could not reach my optimum level of arousal, and, thus, my paper will be on her desk by Friday. I can only console myself with the thought that I am not alone. 10

Procrastinators, however, should take heart. Some of the best things in life wouldn't be the same without procrastination. After all, a 11 good wine isn't a fine wine until it has spent some time in a cool cellar. And a quick stew may be "all right," but a stew that has been procrastinating in the pot all day is worth the wait. The French say that you're not a woman till you're forty—is this procrastination in disguise? As long as people don't procrastinate for too long, good things do come to those who wait.

Works Cited

Plotnic, Rod. *Introduction to Psychology*. Belmont, CA: Brooks/Cole, 1993.
Rathus, Spencer A. *Essentials of Psychology*. New York: Holt, 1989.

BATTERED-WOMAN SYNDROME

Hobi Reader

•

Southwestern College
Chula Vista, California

Battered-woman syndrome. This is the current name for spousal abuse. Before that it was called wife beating. Before that it was called okay. For eons, a woman was considered the possession of a man. Not only was beating a woman accepted, it was also expected in order to keep her under control, to show her who was the boss, and to allow a man to prove his superiority and manliness.

The term *battered-woman syndrome* was coined by Lenore Walker and described in her book *Terrifying Love*. In an earlier book, *The Battered Woman*, she identifies three phases of abuse (49). The first is a tension-building phase, when minor battering occurs. This is followed by an acute battering period, when intensity or frequency increases. The third phase is a calm period, often with the batterer begging for forgiveness and offering gifts and kindness. This is when he usually promises never to hurt the woman again. Even with professional help, however, the abuse usually continues.

Battered-woman syndrome is a very misunderstood concept. Many people are not aware of its widespread existence. Others are not even sure what the term means. Once statistics are reviewed, many are shocked. According to the National Organization for Women, there are more than four million women beaten by their husbands or boyfriends every day in the United States, although most assaults are not reported to law-enforcement agencies. One out of seven women has been repeatedly raped by her partner (United States 3). The statistics for divorced women who no longer live with their abusers show that more than 75 percent of these women are still being battered. The most shocking fact, perhaps, is that there are three times as many animal shelters in this country as there are battered women's shelters.

Many behaviorists compare a battered woman's emotional state to the Stockholm syndrome. This syndrome describes the state of mind of hostages and prisoners who sometimes undergo a bonding with their captors. The hostages become complacent and withdrawn and are often suspicious of anyone who comes to their rescue (Hickey 9). 4

The battered woman is, in effect, brainwashed into believing whatever her captor/husband says. She becomes distrustful of outsiders and increasingly relies on the husband's truths as her own. The woman is a creature created by the batterer. She has been told lies for so long about who she is that the lies become part of her beliefs about herself. She comes to believe that she is stupid, worthless, unable to make decisions for herself, a bad mother, etc., etc. She is so used to being controlled and beaten into submission that she becomes the perfect victim. Everything is her fault. Nothing she does is good enough. And, to make matters worse, the abuser is often so inconsistent with his beatings that the woman lives in a constant state of fear, never knowing what might set him off. This fear creates an incredible amount of stress. And the psychological damage that results creates a prison for the battered woman (Walker, *Terrifying* 49). As one battered woman said, "The bruises and slaps would eventually heal and go away, but I'll never forget the awful things he said about the way I look, the way I cook, and how I take care of the kids" (qtd. in Spouza 1). 5

Many an abuser will not let his wife out of his sight. The woman is confined to the home and not allowed contact with family or friends. The abuser is suspicious of everything—phone calls, mail, looks from other men—even a gesture or look by his wife might mean something is amiss. The man controls all aspects of the woman's life—what she wears, whom she speaks to, where she goes, how much money she gets. The woman comes to feel trapped and powerless. And the man is clearly in control. 6

Often the abuser was himself abused as a child. Many never learned how to deal with their anger. Underneath all this aggressive behavior, there is often a scared and insecure man venting the feelings he has about his own lack of self-esteem. The abuser may never have learned how to feel or express anger without associating his anger with violence (United States 5). Or, he may have seen his father beat his 7 mother. A man may also batter because of socialization and the belief that it is a man's role to dominate the family by any possible means. Although these stereotypical "macho" characteristics are more prevalent in certain cultures, wife beating knows no ethnic boundaries. It is also blind to age, wealth, social standing, religion, and any other diversity of humankind.

Why would a woman enter a relationship such as this? There are many reasons. The first is that the man often doesn't show any violent behavior during the courtship period. He is an expert at manipulation and is often very romantic—the last man she might think could be violent. Another reason is that the woman might think she can change the man if he has already become violent with her. "Once we're married he'll be nicer," she may tell herself. "When the children start coming he'll be better." Or: "He's just stressed out now, once he finds a job he'll stop hitting me. If only I stop talking back so much he won't have to hit me." The battered woman usually makes excuses from the very beginning of an abusive relationship. Often, she has been in a violent home before and knows the signs but chooses to ignore them. In this way, she becomes trapped in a cycle of abuse, feeling she deserves it. She may actually be comforted that she is getting attention from a man, even if it is negative. And so the cycle of abuse continues. 8

Sexual abuse and degradation are common in violent relationships. Rape is very common, and forced copulation with friends of the abuser also occurs. These acts are more than sexual acts; they are in fact about control, with the abuser acting from the need to control every aspect of a woman's life. 9

Why do women remain in these abusive relationships? Many times they remain because they are terrified. They have become the victims of abusers. Walker borrowed the term *learned helplessness* to describe the emotional state of a battered woman. The term was originally used by Martin Seligman to describe the condition of dogs that were electrically shocked at repeated but irregular intervals. The dogs eventually became so broken in spirit that they didn't use opportunities given them to escape (Walker, *Battered* 40). Thus the term *learned helplessness*. 10

The physical injuries suffered by a battered woman are often so severe that they cause bruises, strangle marks, black eyes, broken bones, internal bleeding, miscarriage, brain damage, and death. The emotional injuries are just as severe, if not more so, even if not physically visible. In desperation, a woman may resort to self-defense in order to survive. Sometimes this means that the victim kills her abuser. Unfor- 11 tunately, many of these women who do retaliate against their abusers end up in jail for first-degree murder because of the lack of understanding of our criminal justice system. The children of these women become orphans, their husbands become victims, and, as always, the woman is guilty.

When there are children in the home, there is a 300-percent increase in physical violence by male batterers. These children suffer from a variety of symptoms as well, including psychic, emotional, and physical harm that is irreparable. Many grow up to become batterers themselves or the victims of batterers (NiCarthy 32). 12

Society has begun to change its views on battered women. Once, the cycle of violence was viewed as the woman's fault, just as it was considered the man's right to beat his wife. Through education and public forums, however, the general public is becoming more informed about battered-woman syndrome. This may be the first important step in stopping the cycle of abuse. 13

Works Cited

Hickey, Cheryl. "Battered Woman Syndrome—License to Kill or Self Defense?" *California Now News.* Apr. 1992: 9.

NiCarthy, Ginny. *Getting Free.* Seattle: Seal, 1982.

Spouza, Valerie. *Domestic Violence Info Guide.* San Diego: Junior League of San Diego, San Diego Domestic Violence Council, n.d.

United States. Dept. of Health and Human Services. *Plain Talk.* Washington: GPO, 1993.

Walker, Lenore. *The Battered Woman.* New York: Harper, 1979.

———. *Terrifying Love.* New York: Harper, 1989.

CHAPTER 6

TAKING A POSITION

*W*hen we write to take a position on a controversial subject, our purpose isn't to express ourselves or to inform others; it is to get readers to nod their heads in agreement. The biggest challenge a writer faces when writing argument may be moving outside the limitations of his or her own perspective on an issue. Knowing where readers stand in relation to the subject is as important as knowing where you stand. Finding common ground in values and beliefs allows readers to construct a pathway to agreement. As you read the essays in this chapter, notice how they appeal to such shared values to establish common ground as well as the ways they use evidence and logic to reason toward their conclusions.

Michael Kingston opens his essay, "Creating a Criminal," with logic, clearly establishing the facts and questions that surround an emotionally charged issue that is probably unfamiliar to most readers. Kingston reasons his way through problems he finds in a racially discriminating law and reaches an emotional conclusion that readers are likely to identify with.

Mark Jackson, on the other hand, opens "The Liberal Arts: A Practical View" with an emotional appeal and then moves into logical discussion that draws on both sources and personal experience. At times his emotional tone is dangerously close to alienating readers, but Jackson skillfully incorporates the opposition and actually forges a new position, reflecting a reasoning process that artfully concedes a counterargument, then uses it to temper a compromise.

As you read Brent Knutson's argument for repealing speed limit laws on U.S. interstate highways ("Auto Liberation"), check the roadway he constructs for you to travel on toward assent. This essay offers a good example of argument that expresses a strong position on a controversial topic. While the writer may not succeed at persuading every reader to agree fully with his position, he may nevertheless hope to gain assent on at least a point or two, thereby creating a subtle *movement that might expand common ground and eventually, if not now, gain full assent.*

From the precisely detailed opening scenario, Knutson's essay speaks with authority derived from both personal experience and library research. By so effectively acknowledging opposition to his thesis and confronting it with solid counterargument, the writer puts readers in an interesting, and somewhat difficult, position at the end, especially those readers who started out completely disagreeing with his position. If this is true for you, can you assess the extent Knutson's essay succeeds at creating a shift in your own thinking on the issue? What are you willing to agree with, and why?

Glenna J. Hughes derives authority in her argument almost wholly from her personal experience. By narrating a story that clearly demonstrates the imminent threat posed by a certain class of hunters, she makes a convincing case for the game commission's changing its hunting license regulations. While research could undoubtedly bolster her case, Hughes's reasoning from the strong evidence of personal experience is quite persuasive without it.

CREATING A CRIMINAL

Michael Kingston

■

University of California, Riverside
Riverside, California

In reaction to the Vietnamese-American practice of raising ca- 1
nines for food, Section 598b of the California Penal Code was recently
amended to read as follows:

> (a) Every person is guilty of a misdemeanor who possesses, imports into
> this state, sells, buys, gives away, or accepts any carcass or part of any car-
> cass of any animal traditionally or commonly kept as a pet or compan-
> ion with the sole intent of using or having another person use any part
> of that carcass for food.
> (b) Every person is guilty of a misdemeanor who possesses, imports into
> this state, sells, buys, gives away, or accepts any animal traditionally or
> commonly kept as a pet or companion with the sole intent of killing or
> having another person kill that animal for the purpose of using or hav-
> ing another person use any part of the animal for food.

This is a fascinating new law, one that brings up a complex set of 2
moral, political, and social questions. For example: What constitutes a
"pet"? Do pets have special "rights" that other animals aren't entitled
to? How should these "rights" be balanced with the real political rights
of the human populace? How do we define the civil rights of an ethnic
minority whose actions reflect cultural values that are at odds with those
of the majority? Section 598b does not mention these issues. Rather, it
seems to simply walk around them, leaving us to figure out for ourselves
whose interests (if any) are being served by this strange new law.

95

The first thing one might wonder is whether the purpose of Section 598b is to improve the lot of pets throughout California. What we do know is that it seeks to prevent people from eating animals traditionally regarded as pets (dogs and cats). But for the most part, the only people who eat dogs or cats are Vietnamese-Americans. Furthermore, they don't consider these animals "pets" at all. So, pets aren't really being protected. Maybe Section 598b means to say (in a roundabout manner) that *all* dogs and cats are special and therefore deserve protection. Yet, it doesn't protect them from being "put to sleep" in government facilities by owners who are no longer willing to have them. Nor does it protect them from being subjected to painful, lethal experiments designed to make cosmetics safe for human use. Nor does it protect them from unscrupulous veterinarians who sometimes keep one or two on hand to supply blood for anemic pets of paying customers. No, the new law simply prevents Vietnamese-Americans from using them as food.

Is the consumption of dogs or cats so horrible that it merits its own law? One possible answer is that these practices pose a special threat to the trust that the pet-trading network relies upon. Or in other words: that strange man who buys one or more of *your* puppies might just be one of those dog-eaters. But this scenario just doesn't square with reality. A Vietnamese-American, canine-eating family is no more a threat to the pet-trading industry than is a family of European heritage that chooses to raise rabbits (another popular pet) for its food. Predictably, there is a loophole in Section 598b that allows for the continued eating of pet rabbits. Its circular logic exempts from the new law any animal that is part of an *established* agricultural industry.

It seems as though Vietnamese-Americans are the only ones who can't eat what they want, and so it is hard not to think of the issue in terms of racial discrimination. And why shouldn't we? After all, the Vietnamese community in California has long been subjected to bigotry. Isn't it conceivable that latent xenophobia and racism have found their way into the issue of dog-eating? One needs only to look at the law itself for the answer. This law protects animals "traditionally . . . kept as a pet." *Whose* traditions? Certainly not the Vietnamese's.

Of course, the typical defense for racially discriminatory laws such as this one is that they actually protect minorities by forcing assimilation. The reasoning here is that everything will run much smoother if we can all just manage to fall in step with the dominant culture. This argument has big problems. First, it is morally bankrupt. How does robbing a culture of its uniqueness constitute a protection?

Second, it doesn't defuse racial tensions at all. Racists will always find reasons for hating the Vietnamese. Finally, any policy that seeks to label minorities as the cause of the violence leveled against them is inherently racist itself.

Whatever the motives behind Section 598b, the consequences of the new law are all too clear. The government, not content with policing personal sexual behavior, has taken a large step toward dictating what a person can or cannot eat. This is no small infringement. I may never have the desire to eat a dog, but I'm rankled that the choice is no longer mine, and that the choice was made in a climate of racial intolerance. Whatever happened to the right to life, liberty, and the pursuit of happiness?   7

Unfortunately, we may suffer more than just a reduction in personal choice. Crimes such as dog-eating require a certain amount of vigilance to detect. More than likely, the police will rely upon such dubious measures as sifting through garbage left at curbside, or soliciting anonymous tips. Laws that regulate private behavior, after all, carry with them a reduction in privacy.   8

We sure are giving up a lot for this new law. It's sad that we receive only more criminals in return.   9

THE LIBERAL ARTS: A PRACTICAL VIEW

Mark Jackson

∎

University of Cincinnati
Cincinnati, Ohio

Many students question the reasoning behind a liberal arts education. But even though they may have been forced to swallow liberal arts propaganda since junior high, students seldom receive a good explanation for why they should strive to be "well-rounded." They are told that they should value the accumulation of knowledge for its own sake, yet this argument does not convince those, like myself, who believe that knowledge must have some practical value or material benefit to be worth seeking.

In "What Is an Idea," Wayne Booth and Marshall Gregory argue convincingly that "a liberal education is an education in ideas—not merely memorizing them, but learning to move among them, balancing one against the other, negotiating relationships, accommodating new arguments, and returning for a closer look" (17). These writers propose that a liberal arts education is valuable to students because it helps to develop their analytical-thinking skills and writing skills. This is, perhaps, one of the best arguments for taking a broad range of classes in many different subjects.

Other more radical arguments in favor of the liberal arts are less appealing. Lewis Thomas, a prominent scientist and physician, believes that classical Greek should form the backbone of a college student's education. This suggestion seems extreme. It is more reasonable to concentrate on the English language, since many students do not have a firm grasp of basic reading and writing skills. Freshman English and other English courses serve as a better foundation for higher education than classical Greek could.

The opposition to a liberal arts curriculum grows out of the values that college-bound students learn from their parents and peers: they place an immeasurable value on success and disregard anything that is not pertinent to material achievements. Students often have trouble seeing what practical value studying a particular discipline can have for them. Teenagers who are headed for the world of nine-to-five employment tend to ignore certain studies in their haste to succeed. 4

My parents started discussing the possibility of college with me when I was in the sixth grade. They didn't think that it was important for me to go to college to become a more fulfilled human being. My mom and dad wanted me to go to college so that I might not have to live from paycheck to paycheck like they do. Their reason for wanting me to go to college has become my primary motivation for pursuing a college degree. 5

I remember getting into an argument with my high school counselor because I didn't want to take a third year of Spanish. I was an A student in Spanish II, but I hated every minute of the class. My counselor noticed that I didn't sign up for Spanish III, so he called me into his office to hassle me. I told him that I took two years of a foreign language so that I would be accepted to college, but that I did not want to take a third year. Mr. Gallivan told me that I needed a third year of foreign language to be a "well-rounded" student. My immediate response was "So what?!" I hated foreign languages, and no counselor was going to make me take something that I didn't want or need. I felt Spanish was a waste of time. 6

I frequently asked my high school counselor why I needed to take subjects like foreign languages and art. He never really gave me an answer (except for the lame idea about being "well-rounded"). Instead, Mr. Gallivan always directed my attention to a sign on the wall of his office which read, There's No Reason for It. It's Just Our Policy! I never found that a satisfactory explanation. 7

Norman Cousins, however, does offer a more reasonable explanation for the necessity of a liberal education. In his essay "How to Make People Smaller Than They Are," Cousins points out how valuable the humanities are for career-minded people. He says, "The irony of the emphasis being placed on careers is that nothing is more valuable for anyone who has had a professional or vocational education than to be able to deal with abstractions or complexities, or to feel comfortable 8 with subtleties of thought or language, or to think sequentially" (31). Cousins reminds us that technical or vocational knowledge alone will not make one successful in a chosen profession: unique problems and situations may arise daily in the context of one's job, so an employee must be able to think creatively and deal with events that no textbook ever discussed. The workers who get the promotions and advance to high positions are the ones who can "think on their feet" when they are faced with a complex problem.

Cousins also suggests that the liberal arts teach students communication skills that are critical for success. A shy, introverted person who was a straight A student in college would not make a very good public relations consultant, no matter how keen his or her intellectual abilities. Employees who cannot adequately articulate their ideas to a client or an employer will soon find themselves unemployed, even if they have brilliant ideas. Social integration into a particular work environment would be difficult without good communication skills and a wide range of interests and general knowledge. The broader a person's interests, the more compatible he or she will be with other workers.

Though it is obvious that liberal arts courses do have considerable practical value, a college education would not be complete without some job training. The liberal arts should be given equal billing in the college curriculum, but by no means should they become the focal point of higher education. If specialization is outlawed in our institutions of higher learning, then college students might lose their competitive edge. Maxim Gorky has written that "any kind of knowledge is useful" (264), and, of course, most knowledge *is* useful; but it would be insane to structure the college curriculum around an overview of all disciplines instead of allowing a student to master one subject or profession. Universities must seek to maintain an equilibrium between liberal and specialized education. A liberal arts degree without specialization or intended future specialization (such as a master's degree in a specific field) is useless unless one wants to be a professional game show contestant.

Students who want to make the most of their college years should pursue a major course of study while choosing electives or a few minor courses of study from the liberal arts. In this way, scholars can become experts in a profession and still have a broad enough background to insure versatility, both within and outside the field. In a university's quest to produce "well-rounded" students, specialization must not come to be viewed as an evil practice.

If educators really want to increase the number of liberal arts courses that each student takes, they must first increase the popularity of such studies. It is futile to try to get students to learn something just for the sake of knowing it. They must be given examples, such as those already mentioned, of how a liberal education will further their own interests. Instead of telling students that they need to be "well-rounded" and feeding them meaningless propaganda, counselors and professors should point out the practical value and applications of a broad education in the liberal arts. It is difficult to persuade some college students that becoming a better person is an important goal of higher education. Many students want a college education so that they can make more money and have more power. This is the perceived value of a higher education in their world.

Works Cited

Booth, Wayne, and Marshall Gregory, eds. *The Harper and Row Reader.* 2nd ed. New York: Harper, 1988.

———. "What Is an Idea?" Booth and Gregory 15–18.

Cousins, Norman. "How to Make People Smaller Than They Are." Booth and Gregory 30–32.

Gorky, Maxim. "On Books." Booth and Gregory 255–66.

Thomas, Lewis. "Debating the Unknowable." Booth and Gregory 797–803.

AUTO LIBERATION

Brent Knutson

∎

Boise State University
Boise, Idaho

The driver of a late-model Japanese sports car grins as he 1
downshifts into third gear, blips the throttle with his heel, and releases
the clutch. The car's rear end abruptly steps out in the wide, sweeping
corner. He cranks the wheel, gathering the tail while eagerly stabbing
the accelerator. The engine emits a metallic wail and barks angrily as
the driver pulls the gearshift into fourth. Controlled pandemonium
ensues as the secondary turbocharger engages and slams the driver's cranium against the headrest. With adrenaline thumping in his temples,
he watches the needle on the speedometer sweep urgently toward the
end of the scale. The driver then flicks the turn signal and blasts onto
the interstate like a guided missile launching from a fighter jet. Today,
he will not be late for work.

This scenario may seem a bit far-fetched, enough so that one 2
might conclude that the driver is unnecessarily risking his life and the
lives of other people on the road. But, on Germany's autobahns, people normally drive in excess of 80 miles per hour. Yet, these German
superhighways are the safest in the world, filled with German drivers
who are skilled, competent, and courteous. Using the autobahn system
as a model, it is possible to examine whether national speed limits in
the United States are necessary.

In fact, there is solid reasoning to support the claim that the speed 3
limits on U.S. interstate highways should be repealed. Not only are

American speed limits unnecessarily restrictive, they also infringe upon the personal freedoms of American citizens. Although there are locations where speed limits are appropriate, in most cases these limits are arbitrarily imposed and sporadically enforced. Modern automobiles are capable of traveling safely at high speeds, and, despite what the auto-insurance consortium would have us believe, speed does not kill. With proper training, American drivers could be capable of driving "at speed" responsibly. Perhaps the most compelling reason to lift the national speed limit is the simplest: driving fast is enjoyable.

Those opposed to lifting the national speed limit argue that re-   4 moving such restrictions would result in mayhem on the freeway; they're convinced that the countryside would be littered with the carcasses of people who achieved terminal velocity only to careen off the road and explode into flames. Speed limit advocates also argue that American drivers do not possess the skill or capacity to drive at autobahn speeds. They contend that our driver-education programs do not sufficiently prepare drivers to operate vehicles, and obtaining a driver's license in most states is comically easy; therefore, lifting the speed limit would be irresponsible.

The belief that a "no speed limit" highway system would result   5 in widespread carnage appears to be based more on fear than fact. In 1987, Idaho Senator Steve Symms introduced legislation allowing states to raise speed limits on rural interstates to 65 miles per hour (Csere, "Free" 9). Auto-insurance industry advocates responded that the accident rates would skyrocket and the number of fatalities caused by auto accidents would increase accordingly. Ironically, the Insurance Institute for Highway Safety (IIHS) reported in July 1994 that "[o]nly 39,235 deaths resulting from auto-related accidents were reported during 1992, the lowest number since 1961. The institute found that 1992 was the fourth year in which automotive deaths consistently declined" (qtd. in "Highways" 51). Coincidentally, that decline in fatalities began two years after many states raised interstate speed limits. Unfortunately, the insurance industry has made it a habit to manipulate statistics to suit its purposes. Later in the essay, I'll discuss evidence of this propensity to deceive.

The contention that American drivers are not capable of driving   6 safely at higher speeds has some merit. During a drive around any city in this country, one is bound to witness numerous displays of behind-the-wheel carelessness. Because of poor driver-education programs, as well as general apathy, Americans have earned their standing among the worst drivers in the world. Regarding our poor driving habits, automotive journalist Csaba Csere wrote in the April 1994 issue of *Car and Driver:* "American drivers choose their lanes randomly, much in the way cows inexplicably pick a patch of grass on which to graze" ("Drivers" 9). Fortunately, Americans' poor driving habits can be remedied. Through intensive driver-education programs, stringent licensing criteria, and public-service announcement campaigns, we can learn to drive more proficiently.

I recently returned from a four-year stay in Kaiserslautern, Germany. While there, I learned the pleasure of high-speed motoring. I was particularly impressed by the skill and discipline demonstrated by virtually all drivers traveling on the network of superhighways that make up the autobahn system. Germany's automobile regulatory laws are efficient, practical, and serve as an example for all countries to follow. It is striking that automobiles and driving fast are such integral components of German culture. Germans possess a passion for cars that is so contagious I didn't want to leave the country. German Chancellor Helmut Kohl summed up the German attitude regarding speed limits quite concisely: "For millions of people, a car is part of their personal freedom" (qtd. in Cote 12).

It is apparent in the United States that there are not many old, junky cars left on the road. The majority of vehicles operating in the United States are newer cars that have benefited from automotive engineering technology designed to increase the performance of the average vehicle. With the advent of independent suspension, electronic engine-management systems, passive restraints, and other technological improvements, modern automobiles are more capable than ever of traveling at high speeds, safely. Indeed, the stringent safety requirements imposed by the Department of Transportation for vehicles sold in the United States ensures that our cars and trucks are the safest in the world.

One of the biggest fallacies perpetrated by the auto-insurance industry and car-fearing legislators is that "speed kills." Driving fast in itself, however, is not a hazard; speed combined with incompetence, alcohol, or hazardous conditions is dangerous. A skilled motor-vehicle operator traveling at 90 miles per hour, in light traffic, on a divided highway does not present a significant risk. Psychologist and compensation theorist G. J. Wilde "developed the RHT (Risk Homeostasis Theory) to account for the apparent propensity of drivers to maintain a constant level of experienced accident risk" (qtd. in Jackson and Blackman 950). During a driving simulation experiment in which he changed "non-motivational factors," Wilde determined that "Neither speed limit nor speeding fine had a significant impact on accident loss" (qtd. in Jackson and Blackman 956). Wilde's theory is convincing because he emphasizes the human tendency towards self-preservation. The impact of RHT could be far-reaching. As Wilde says, "The notion that drivers compensate fully for non-motivational safety countermeasures is significant because it is tantamount to the claim that most legislated safety measures will not permanently reduce the total population traffic accident loss" (qtd. in Jackson and Blackman 951). What this means is that drivers would not increase their personal risk by driving faster than their capabilities dictate, regardless of the speed limit.

Unfortunately, the IIHS doesn't see things this way. They have been busy manipulating statistics in an attempt to convince people that raising the interstate speed limits to 65 miles per hour has resulted in a veritable bloodbath. A headline in a recent edition of the IIHS status report states, "For Sixth Year in a Row, Deaths on U.S. Rural Interstates Are Much Higher Than before Speed Limits Were Raised to 65 mph" (qtd. in Bedard 205). That statistic is more than a little misleading because it does not compensate for the increased number of drivers on the road. Patrick Bedard explains: "What's the real conclusion? Rural interstate fatalities over the whole United States increased 19 percent between 1982 and 1992. But driving increased 44 percent. So the fatality rate is on a definite downward trend from 1.5 to 1.2 [percent]" (21). 10

One might ask what the insurance industry stands to gain by misrepresenting auto fatality statistics. The real issue is what they stand to lose if speed limits are deregulated. The lifting of speed limits translates into fewer traffic citations issued by police. Fewer tickets means fewer points assessed on Americans' driving records, which would remove the insurance industry's primary tool for raising premiums. Needless to say, they aren't thrilled about the prospect of less money in their coffers. 11

There is one lucid and persuasive argument to abolish interstate speed limits: Driving fast is pure, unadulterated, rip-snortin' fun. I experienced the thrill of a lifetime behind the wheel of a 1992 Ford Mustang while chasing a BMW 525i on the Frankfurt-Mainz Autobahn. I remember my heart racing as I glanced at my speedometer, which read 120 mph. When I looked up, I saw the high-beam flash of headlights in my rearview mirror. Moments after I pulled into the right lane, a bloodred Ferrari F-40 passed in a surreal symphony of sound, color, and power, dominated by the enraged howl of a finely tuned Italian motor at full tilt. At that moment, I was acutely aware of every nerve ending 12 in my body, as I experienced the automotive equivalent of Zen consciousness. It was a sort of convergence of psyche and body that left me light-headed and giddy for ten minutes afterwards. I was glad to discover that my reaction to driving fast was not unique:

> Few people can describe in words the mixture of sensations they experience, but for some the effect is so psychologically intense that no other experience can match it. . . . For some people the psychological effects are experienced as pure fear. For others, however, this basic emotional state is modified to give a sharply tingling experience which is perceived as intensely pleasurable. The fear, and the state of alertness are still there — but they have been mastered (Marsh and Collett 179).

Repealing interstate speed limits is an objective that every driver 13 should carefully consider. At a time when our elected officials are striving to control virtually every aspect of our lives, it is imperative that we fight to regain our freedom behind the wheel. Like Germans, Americans have a rich automotive culture and heritage. The automobile represents our ingenuity, determination, and independence. It is time to return control of the automobile to the driver, and "free us from our speed slavery once and for all" (Csere, "Free" 9).

Works Cited

Bedard, Patrick. "Auto Insurance Figures Don't Lie, but Liars Figure." Editorial. *Car and Driver* Mar. 1994: 20–21.

Cote, Kevin. "Heartbrake on Autobahn." *Advertising Age* 26 Sept. 1994: 1+.

Csere, Csaba. "Drivers We Love to Hate." Editorial. *Car and Driver* Apr. 1994: 9.

———. "Free the Speed Slaves." Editorial. *Car and Driver* Nov. 1993: 9.

"Highways Become Safer." *Futurist* Jan.–Feb. 1994: 51–52.

Jackson, Jeremy S. H., and Roger Blackman. "A Driving Simulator Test of Wilde's Risk Homeostasis Theory." *Journal of Applied Psychology* 79.6 (1994): 950–58.

Marsh, Peter, and Peter Collett. *Driving Passion*. Winchester: Faber, 1987.

Abolish Lifetime Hunting Licenses for People over Sixty-Five

Glenna J. Hughes

·

Westmoreland County Community College
Youngwood, Pennsylvania

Grandpa was mowing the grass on a beautiful, warm sum- 1
mer day when, all at once, he began to have one of his episodes: yelling
at the trees, he wandered the neighborhood looking for Grandma and
Aunt Stella. Poor Grandpa. Grandma and Aunt Stella died in a traffic
accident over fourteen years ago.

This is an all-too-real scenario. As the aging process begins, men- 2
tal processes slow down. Some elderly people, while not diagnosed as
senile or as suffering from Alzheimer's or arteriosclerotic heart disease,
still exhibit many of the same symptoms: forgetting where they are, why
they are there, what they are doing. The confusion associated with
aging can at times be severe.

October 30, 1988. This cool, crisp autumn day a forty-year-old 3
husband and father of two is walking a tram road in Rockwood, Pennsylvania. He and his father are turkey hunting, and he's disappointed
that he hasn't seen any turkeys. At 12:15 P.M., he decides it's time to
head back to the truck to meet his dad and get some lunch. As he turns,
he hears a gunshot. He feels a stinging on his face, and then the pain;
he realizes he has been shot. Looking in the direction of the shot, he
yells, "Get help! I've been shot! Please, get help!" Then, he sees the second shot fired, the smoke and the shell packing coming out of the gun.
He pulls the stock of his own gun in front of his face; he feels the stinging of the buckshot, and everything turns red. Wondering if he is going

to live or die, he begins to run in the opposite direction from the gun-shots. Covered with blood, he flags a passing train. The engineer ra-dioes for a truck to take him out of the woods to a waiting ambulance.

That dear old grandpa who suffered confusion while cutting his   4
grass *has a lifetime hunting license from the Pennsylvania State Game Com-mission.* No one from the game commission had any idea that Grandpa was having a little trouble with his hearing, that his eyesight wasn't what it used to be, or that he suffered episodes of confusion. All the com-mission knew was that he had reached his sixty-fifth birthday and had the $50.75 to pay for a lifetime hunting license in Pennsylvania.

I believe that rather than becoming eligible for a lifetime license,   5
every hunter over the age of sixty-five should be required to report to an agent of the game commission each year. They should present a doc-tor's statement describing their physical and mental condition, and the agent for the commission should conduct a vision and hearing test and administer a written hunter-safety test. The commission already re-quires adolescent hunters to participate in hunter-safety classes and to hunt with an adult until the age of sixteen. If the commission recog-nizes the need to monitor young hunters, then why can't it accept the need to monitor elderly hunters?

I realize that people do not all age at the same rate: some can begin   6
to be confused in their early fifties, while others have a clear mind well past their eighties. And I'm not saying that every person over the age of sixty-five should be removed from the woods. I am saying that there need to be limits and guidelines for securing the license that gives one permission to carry a shotgun or rifle. The game commission needs to understand that as people get older, their minds get older too. The fact that a man has hunted for forty-five or fifty years doesn't mean that at the age of seventy or eighty he always knows what he's doing. If there is any doubt about the mental or physical condition of a person apply-ing for or renewing a hunting license, that person should be denied a license, and the family notified. Confused and forgetful elderly people cannot be allowed to walk around in the woods with loaded guns; they must be made to relinquish their right to hunt for their own safety and the safety of other hunters.

You see, that forty-year-old father of two was my husband. Today,   7
he is walking around with buckshot in his face and upper body. Only the fact that he wore glasses kept the buckshot from entering the soft spots under his eyes. The dear old grandpa who shot my husband was eighty-three. His family admitted to the police and the game commis-sion that he had been a little "strange" for about ten years. His defense

at the trial was that he was "confused." He admitted that he shot my husband on purpose, that he knew my husband was not a turkey, but he pleaded that he suffered long bouts of disorientation, that in his severe confusion he couldn't remember the police reading him his rights.

A person like Grandpa makes it dangerous to go into the woods. How many others just like him are out there? Would you like to meet him next turkey season? Or how about during deer season, when the rifle he is carrying is a 30.06?

8

CHAPTER 7

PROPOSING SOLUTIONS

*T**he** essays in this chapter show what writers can do when they know their subject and audience well. Three of the essays — "Wheelchair Hell: A Look at Campus Accessibility," "The Waller Times," and "WSU Dining Facilities" — focus on campus problems about which the writers have firsthand knowledge. The fourth essay, "The Road to Acme Looniversity," is broader and less serious in scope, but nevertheless reveals a writer who is thoroughly familiar with both her subject and her audience.*

In some cases, persuading readers that a problem exists is the writer's primary task. In her essay, "Wheelchair Hell: A Look at Campus Accessibility," Shannon Long must first make readers aware, and then get them to accept, that the partial measures for wheelchair accessibility thus far adopted at her university simply do not solve the problem of access for students with disabilities. As a disabled student herself, she is able to use personal experience to make her point quite effectively.

In her essay, "The Road to Acme Looniversity," Kirsten Dockendorff takes a tongue-in-cheek approach to the assignment and winds up with a glowing example of how to reason through a problem, albeit ironically, to reach a plausible solution. While humor works strongly in the writer's favor in this example, we should recognize that the humor works — indeed, that the essay even makes sense — only if readers are familiar with the "Road Runner" cartoon from Warner Brothers' Looney Toons. The writer assumes her audience will have this bit of general cultural knowledge. What happens if they don't? You might think about and discuss how the essay would play for readers if that were the case.

Aimee Crickmore's essay, "The Waller Times," makes different assumptions about its audience. The essay has the flavor of an "op-ed" piece that appears on the editorial pages of local newspapers. The challenge in writing for a local audience of this nature is to know the assumptions, values, and objections that readers hold—in Crickmore's case, the readers in small-town Waller, Texas. By skillfully recategorizing the problem of teen pregnancy as a problem centered in the parents of teenagers rather than in the teenagers themselves, Crickmore hopes to convince the residents of Waller that a fresh solution is necessary to solve a long-standing problem.

The audience that Richard Blake assumes for his essay, "WSU Dining Facilities," is probably aware that problems exist with the campus food service but may not be aware of the extent of student dissatisfaction. Blake's survey allows him to define the problem more precisely and thus approach its source more realistically. Although he recognizes that the real source of the dining-facility problem is a lack of competition, he is wise enough to see that the situation is unlikely to change unless students make their opinions publicly known. The solution Blake proposes is a simple one, but, as is the case with much in the realm of public policy, it is far from simplistic. In calling for students to act on their complaints, the writer takes on the difficult role of community organizer.

WHEELCHAIR HELL: A LOOK AT CAMPUS ACCESSIBILITY

Shannon Long

■

University of Kentucky
Lexington, Kentucky

It was my first week of college, and I was going to the library   1
to meet someone on the third floor and study. After entering the library,
I went to the elevator and hit the button calling it. A few seconds later
the doors opened, I rolled inside, and the doors closed behind me. Expecting the buttons to be down in front, I suddenly noticed that they
were behind me—and too high to reach. There I was stuck in the elevator with no way to get help. Finally, somebody got on at the fourth
floor. I'd been waiting fifteen minutes.

I'm not the only one who has been a victim of inaccessibility. The   2
University of Kentucky currently has twelve buildings that are inaccessible to students in wheelchairs (Karnes). Many other buildings, like
the library, are accessible, but have elevators that are inoperable by
handicapped students. Yet, Section 504 of the Rehabilitation Act of
1973 states that

> No qualified handicapped person shall, because a recipient's facilities are
> inaccessible to or unusable by handicapped persons, be denied the ben-
> efits of, be excluded from participation in, or otherwise be subjected to
> discrimination under any program or activity receiving Federal financial
> assistance (*Federal* 22681).

When this law went into effect in 1977, the University of Ken-   3
tucky started a renovation process in which close to a million dollars
was spent on handicap modifications (Karnes). But even though that

much money has been spent, there are still many more modifications needed. Buildings still inaccessible to wheelchair students are the Administration Building, Alumni House, Barker Hall, Bowman Hall, Bradley Hall, Engineering Quadrangle, Gillis Building, Kinkead Hall, Miller Hall, Safety and Security Building, and Scovell Hall (University).

So many inaccessible buildings creates many unnecessary problems. For example, if a handicapped student wants to meet an administrator, he or she must make an appointment to meet somewhere more accessible than the Administration Building. Making appointments is usually not a problem, but there is still the fact that able-bodied students have no problem entering the Administration Building while handicapped students cannot. Though handicapped students can enter the Gillis Building, they cannot go above the ground floor and even have to push a button to get someone to come downstairs to help them. Finally, for handicapped students to get counseling from the Career Planning Center, they must set up an appointment to meet with someone at another place. In this case, some students might not use the center's services because of the extra effort involved (Croucher).   4

Even many of the accessible buildings have elevators, water fountains, and door handles that are inoperable by handicapped students (Karnes). Elevators in the library and Whitehall Classroom Building, for instance, have buttons too high for wheelchair students, forcing them to ask somebody else to hit the button. If there is nobody around to ask, the handicapped person simply has to wait. In the Chemistry and Physics Building, a key is needed to operate the elevator, forcing wheelchair students to ride up and down the hall to find somebody to help. Many water fountains are inaccessible to people in wheelchairs. Some buildings have only *one* accessible water fountain. Finally, hardly any buildings have doorknobs that students with hand and arm impairments can operate.   5

Many residence halls, such as Boyd Hall, Donovan Hall, Patterson Hall, and Keenland Hall, are also completely inaccessible. If a handicapped student wanted to drop by and see a friend or attend a party in one of these dorms, he or she would have to be carried up steps. Kirivan and Blanding Towers have bathrooms that are inaccessible. Also, in Kirivan Tower the elevator is so small that someone has to lift the back of the chair into the elevator. The complex low-rises—Shawneetown, Commonwealth Village, and Cooperstown Apartments—are also inaccessible. Cooperstown has some first-floor apartments that are accessible, but a handicapped student couldn't very well live there because the bathrooms are inaccessible. All eleven sororities are inaccessible, and   6 only five of the sixteen fraternities are accessible. Since the land sororities and fraternities are on is owned by UK, Section 504 does require that houses be accessible (University 14, 15).

With so many UK places still inaccessible, it is obvious that hundreds of modifications need to be done. According to Jake Karnes, the assistant dean of students and the director of Handicap Student Services, "It will probably take close to a million dollars to make UK totally accessible." UK's current budget allows for just $10,000 per year to go toward handicap modification (Karnes). If no other money source is sought, the renovation process could be strung out for many years.

A possible solution could be the use of the tuition. If only $2 could be taken from each student's tuition, there would be almost $50,000 extra per semester for handicap modification. Tuition is already used to pay for things ranging from teacher salaries to the funding of the campus radio station. This plan could be started with the beginning of the fall semester. The money could be taken from each of the existing programs the tuition now pays for, so there would be no need for an increase in tuition. Also, this would not be a permanent expense because with an extra $50,000 a semester, all of the needed modifications could be finished in ten years. After that, the amount taken from the tuition could be lowered to fifty cents to help cover upkeep of campus accessibility. This plan is practical — but more important, it is ethical. Surely if part of our tuition goes to fund a radio station, some of it can be used to make UK a more accessible place. Which is more important, having a radio station to play alternative music or having a campus that is accessible to all students?

June 1980 was the deadline for meeting the requirements of Section 504 (Robinson 28). In compliance with the law, the University of Kentucky has spent almost a million dollars making its campus more accessible. But there are still many more changes needed. These changes will take a lot of money, but if $2 could be used out of each student's tuition, the money would be there. Handicapped students often work to overachieve to prove their abilities. All they ask for is a chance, and that chance should not be blocked by high buttons, heavy doors, or steps.

Works Cited

Croucher, Lisa. "Accessibility at UK for Handicapped Still Can Be Better." *Kentucky Kernal*. Date unknown.

Federal Register. Vol. 42. 4 May 1977: 22681.

Karnes, Jake. Personal interview. 17 Oct. 1989.

Robinson, Rita. "For the Handicapped: Renovation Report Card." *American School & University* (Apr. 1980): 28.

University of Kentucky. Transition Plan. Report. Date unknown.

The Road to Acme Looniversity

Kirsten Dockendorff

Bowling Green State University
Bowling Green, Ohio

With a "click," the television set goes on. You hear that fa- 1
miliar music and see the Warner Brothers logo indicating it's time for
Looney Toons. We've all watched them, including the many episodes of
Wyle E. Coyote and his never-ending quest to catch the Road Runner.
Secretly, we've all wanted Wyle E. to succeed, although long before the
end of every episode we know that his hard work will only be rewarded
by his being dropped from a cliff, smashed by a falling rock, *and* run
over by a truck. As if that's not bad enough, Wyle E.'s defeat is also made
more miserable by the Road Runner driving over him with his tongue
stuck out and a shrill "Beep! Beep!" One thing is clear: Wyle E. has a
problem, and it is time for him to solve it.

One of the easiest ways to get rid of the bird would be for Wyle 2
E. to hire an assassin. This way, he could rest easily knowing a professional was at work. Wyle E. could use the money usually spent on Acme
products to cover the assassin's fee. This would also save additional
money because Wyle E. would no longer have to buy Acme equipment
or pay all of those expensive hospital bills that result when the Acme
equipment fails. A professional would be a quick, easy, and cost-effective
solution. The major drawback is that Wyle E. would miss the satisfaction of doing the job himself. After so many years of working so hard
to catch the Road Runner, he might want to be part of the event.

A better way for Wyle E. to kill the Road Runner and still par- 3

116

ticipate might be to get some help from his friends. Wyle E. could call on Elmer Fudd, Yosemite Sam, Sylvester the Cat, and Taz, the Tasmanian Devil. By constructing a plan in which he and his friends combine their natural talents, Wyle E. would have the satisfaction of being part of the bird's demise. Taz, with speed equal to the Road Runner's, could chase the bird into a trap designed by Yosemite Sam: a small mound of birdseed in the Road Runner's path. When the bird stops to eat, a cage would drop. Then Sylvester's natural bird-catching instincts could be of use in disabling the bird to prevent escape, perhaps by breaking its legs. After that, Elmer could use his extraordinary hunting skills to finish him off. The only flaw in this plan might be that his friends don't have much of a record of success: Elmer, Sam, and Taz have never caught Bugs Bunny; Sylvester has never caught Tweety; and you know the results of all Wyle E.'s plans. The chance would thus seem infinitesimal at best that even together they might catch the Road Runner.

Wyle E.'s major problem in his pursuit of the Road Runner never seems to be the plan itself, but the products he uses to carry out the plan. None of the equipment he buys from Acme ever works correctly. It may work fine in a test run, but when the Road Runner actually falls into the trap, everything goes crazy or fails completely. In one recurring episode, Wyle E. buys a rocket and a pair of roller skates. His plan is to strap the rocket to his back and the skates to his feet, and thus overtake his speedy prey. The test run is fine. Then the bird runs by, and Wyle E. starts the rocket, which immediately runs out of fuel, blows up, or does not go off. If Wyle E. used a company other than Acme, he might avoid the injuries he suffers from faulty Acme equipment. Of course, one obstacle to this plan is the cost of doing business with a new company. Since Wyle E. probably receives a sizable discount from Acme because of his preferred customer status, he perhaps would not get the same treatment from a new company, at least for a while. On his cartoon-character salary, Wyle E. may not be able to afford higher prices. 4

Given the range of possibilities for catching the Road Runner, the best solution to the problem might be for Wyle E. to use his superior intellect. Wyle E. could undoubtedly convince the Road Runner that a dramatic death scene on the show might win him an Emmy. Since roadrunners are known for their vanity, this Road Runner would seem likely to leap at the prospect of winning fame and fortune for his fine acting skills. With such a prestigious award, the Road Runner could do what every actor dreams of doing: direct. He would win not only fame and fortune, but the respect of his hero, Big Bird. 5

If and when Wyle E. catches the Road Runner, the cartoon, of   6
course, would end. Although this might at first seem tragic, the consequences are really not tragic at all. Wyle E. would have more time to
pursue his movie career and perhaps even teach at Acme Looniversity.
He would have more time to devote to his family, friends, and fans. And
he could finally stop paying a therapist since his psychological issues
would be resolved. Wyle E. would gain self-confidence and no longer
doubt his ability as he did when the birdbrain outsmarted him. He
would finally recognize his own genius and realize his lifelong dream
of opening a theme restaurant.

After years and years of torment and humiliation, it is time for   7
Wyle E. Coyote to catch the Road Runner. Although it is feasible for
Wyle E. to pay an assassin to kill the bird, to enlist his friends for help,
or to stop using Acme products, the best solution is for Wyle E. to use
the immeasurable power of his brain to trick the imbecilic bird. Regardless of the method Wyle E. chooses, one thing is clear: the bird
must *die!*

THE WALLER TIMES

Aimee Crickmore

■

University of Houston
Houston, Texas

Waller, Texas, is a small town far from all other forms of civilization. There is no movie theater, no bowling alley, and certainly no mall. This place doesn't even have a Wal-Mart. Residents of Waller have all heard the saying at least once: "There are only two things for kids to do in Waller, and one of them is drinkin'." This may seem humorous at first, but, unfortunately, there is some truth to it.   1

Teenage pregnancy is one of the biggest problems in Waller. I graduated from high school with 155 other students. On our graduation day, twelve of them were already mothers—two of whom were expecting a second child; and five were expecting their first. Seventeen students in all were pregnant while in high school, and those are just the ones that stayed long enough to graduate! These figures seem astronomical for such a small community, and they represent a significant problem. One result is the necessity for an on-campus day-care center at the high school, which was established in 1992, and, unfortunately, has been growing ever since.   2

The Waller school system has been trying to combat the dilemma for years. I cannot say how long the teen pregnancy problem has existed in Waller, nor how long the school system has been struggling with it, but I do know that the situation has been like this ever since I started junior high school more than six years ago. One of the strategies that educators have used to help curb the pregnancy rate has been   3 to bring in speakers to lecture students on the importance of abstinence as well as safe sex, including discussion of topics ranging from pregnancy to HIV.

Another strategy has been providing students with sex-education 4 courses. I can report that I was privileged to be a part of the "guinea pig" class the school administration chose to use for the sex-education experiment. Let me say, firsthand, that some of the videos shown in sex-education classes were horrifying. People with AIDS spoke about their experiences and of the pain they were suffering. Thirteen-year-old mothers shared their difficulties raising children at such a young age. Young women who had chosen abortion told of the psychological effects they experienced after terminating a pregnancy. Sex-education classes in the Waller public schools have been in full swing for four years, yet, the number of unplanned pregnancies among teenagers is still high.

I suppose the thinking behind this strategy was to scare students 5 into abstinence by bringing to life the straight talk of speakers who had experienced the consequences of irresponsible sex. Unfortunately, fear does not always work on teenagers who truly believe they are invincible. As a result, it seems a different approach is necessary.

A primary cause of teen pregnancy is the fact that many parents 6 do not know *how* to talk to their children about sex and sexual behavior. If parents today were given "lessons" on how to handle the inevitable situation that every parent must sooner or later face, they would be better prepared when the time comes. Many parents are unsure about *when* they should talk with their children about sex. I propose that the school district's next target in the attempt to educate teenagers about sex be the parents. Literature directed to parents regarding teen sex could be sent by mail to parents to heighten their awareness of the issues. Lectures, workshops, and classes could be offered to parents on how to approach the subject of safe and responsible sex.

Trained professionals from the community, including those same 7 ones hired to speak to the students, could also teach the parents. More economically, there are other resources within the community, such as ministers from local churches, who could offer guidance to parents on the ways to speak to children about intimate subjects. Mature high school mothers have said that they would be willing to talk to parents about what they felt was missing from the parental guidance they received, guidance that might have changed the course of their lives.

The Waller community must also think realistically about the 8 problem if any solution is going to work. I know from past experiences with Waller High School that you can talk all you want, but talk is often not translated into action. For this reason, it is important that a committee be formed as soon as possible. Such a committee could consist of students, teachers, administrators, and concerned parents. The committee would be in charge of developing a program and recruiting speakers. Most importantly, the committee must be dedicated to solving what has proven to be a complex and difficult problem. Nothing will get done with half-hearted volunteers.

Not all parents, of course, are going to take the time to commit 9 to this sort of action. If concerned people take the steps necessary to get parents involved, however, maybe the community will wake up to see the depth of this pressing problem. The question of whether the Waller school system should establish a clinic that distributes contraceptives, for instance, as other schools around the country have already done, is a difficult one that needs to be discussed. Waller is a small, country town that would perhaps be uncomfortable with such a big jump that places responsibility for a solution almost entirely in the hands of students. The solution of getting parents involved by offering them resources, support, and education may be a more attractive and reasonable approach. To be frank, strategies that have focused directly on students have failed.

Since election for new school board members is approaching, I 10 would urge the tax-paying citizens of Waller County to attend the next school-board meeting and question board members about the issue of teenage pregnancy and its prevention. After all, residents of Waller all know that unplanned pregnancy is a major problem, and it's only getting worse.

WSU DINING FACILITIES

Richard Blake

▪

Wright State University
Dayton, Ohio

When I was a waiter at a local pizza parlor, the area man- [1]
ager would come in once every two weeks and give the restaurant an
inspection. He would watch us through the course of an evening, and
when the crowds subsided, he would gather us all around and give us
our review. At the onset of every debriefing, as they were called among
the crew, the first words from his mouth would always be, "From the
moment the customer enters those doors, his dining experience begins.
He will form an opinion in his mind about us, and it is your job to make
sure that opinion is good! If it isn't, I'll know about it, and then so will
you."

Even though my experiences at that restaurant are a year behind [2]
me, whenever I eat out I always keep in mind the customer's opinion—
especially when *I* am the customer. When Wright State students eat at
the campus facilities, they form opinions about their dining experience
just as any customer would, and whether that opinion is good or bad is
the responsibility of the food service. Recently I conducted a survey to
determine the student opinion of the food service at Wright State. My
purpose was simply to see if the students were satisfied with the overall performance of Service America, the catering company that handles
all of the campus dining facilities.

I surveyed fifty students over a period of two days at different [3] times and locations. All of those I surveyed ate at least occasionally at one of the dining facilities. The survey rated such aspects as variety, quality, and taste of the food offered as well as the student's opinion of the prices they paid and overall service they received. The ratings given were initially somewhat mediocre.

When rating the food's variety, quality, and taste separately, 67.3 percent rated them as fair, with 13.3 percent rating them as excellent and 19.3 percent rating them as poor. As far as the price of the food was concerned, 54 percent thought it was higher than average, while 46 percent thought it was average. No one said it was lower than average. Overall service was viewed as fair by 60 percent, with 20 percent calling it either excellent or poor.

These results might lead one to believe that there are no strong student complaints with the food services at Wright State, assuming of course that only an overall rating of fair is considered adequate by both the students and the university. However, as I explored the results further I discovered somewhat different conclusions. Of the individuals surveyed, 56 percent felt strong enough in their opinions, either good or bad, to make comments in the space provided at the bottom of the survey. Seventy-five percent of these comments were negative!

What makes these results so important is the fact that such a large number of those surveyed felt strong enough to make comments at all, and that the majority of those comments were negative. Furthermore, those with negative comments accounted for an average of about 40 percent of the fair and average ratings on the overall survey and only about 68 percent of the poor ratings. This means that there are a number of people who have distinct complaints about the food service but rate it as fair anyway. It is perhaps acceptable in this case then to equate fair ratings with somewhat less than adequate performance on the part of the Wright State food service.

So exactly what sort of problems do the students at Wright State have with the food service, and how serious are they? The range of comments I received on my survey was fairly wide, starting with general opinions such as "we're humans, not pigs," to more specific instances of dissatisfaction such as "I have received food . . . more than once . . . with mold on it!" As far as students' overall attitude toward the food service, the comments assumed a similar pattern, from "at least the food is safe" to "do *not* give Service America the 10-year contract." I take such comments as evidence of dissatisfaction with Service America.

The specific complaints I received often dealt with multiple instances of receiving cold food or hard, stale buns on sandwiches, but the two largest categories of discontent were low food quality and slow, unfriendly service. One particular student summed up his feelings by saying, "[The wait] is ridiculous for *fair* food!" So then, if these are the problems, what are the causes?

9

Some students may have the answer to that question already. Twelve percent of the negative respondents felt that Service America has a monopoly at WSU. I assert that this monopoly is the reason for their problems with the food service. A monopoly does exist, at least in respect to the dining facilities, since all of the on-campus eateries (Allyn, The Bike, The Ratt and the UC) are controlled by Service America. No matter where students go to eat on campus, their money goes to the same place. There is no competition on campus to threaten Service America's profits, and therefore there is no particular reason for them to do better than fair in their performance.

10

The problem, then, is the lack of competition. What are some solutions? One solution might be to change catering companies. There are four catering companies that provide this particular type of service to universities and businesses in the area, including Marriot, ARA, Cardinal, and Service America.

11

This solution is oversimplified at best, considering the real problem doesn't necessarily lie with the company itself, but instead with its motivation for performance. Whatever company came in and took over the reins left by Service America would be in the same position as Service America is now! The new company would have yet another monopoly and would be lacking the same competitive drive to perform that the present establishment does.

12

The next answer would then be to create a competitive market at Wright State. Invite several catering services to put up their shingles at Wright State, or even better, forget the catering companies altogether and create a food-court setup like the one at the Dayton Mall. This would create the competitive market needed to keep the various companies on their toes. Every company would be in constant competition with the others, trying to outdo one another in price and service to attract business, and thus profits. It seems almost characteristic of "mall food service operations [to do] everything from tinkering with menus to staging elaborate cross-promotions in order to persuade . . . adults . . . to decide to grab a bite to eat" (Goodman 30). If appealing to consumers were important to compete, students would perhaps get the variety and quality in their meals they don't now have.

However, this utopian view is not feasible for several reasons. The first is that Wright State lacks the room for such a setup, and it is presently involved in so many other projects (such as the Nutter Center and the theater addition) that it cannot make any accommodations. It would also require a large capital investment by other companies to either build this space themselves or renovate preexisting (but unavailable) space. Perhaps the major reason why this setup is not feasible lies with the viewpoints of the companies themselves. Wright State is a commuter school, and the largest number of students have their own transportation (RTA riders not considered). The students are then free to travel wherever they want for meals. They are not restricted as are the students of such schools as Ohio State or University of Cincinnati, both primarily residential schools (which, coincidentally, do have mall food-court setups).

14

There are also other major considerations of policy and profit involved. If a company, say McDonald's, was to build within the university, they would be first limiting themselves to only the WSU community at large for patronage, and secondly submitting themselves to some control and restrictions by Wright State policy. If they build across the street, however, as they have, they are open to the *entire* community of Fairborn (WSU being a part of that community) and subject only to their own control and restrictions. Most other companies adopt a similar view, and in fact are even advised against setting up shop inside facilities they do not own. Chicago-based restaurant consultant John C. Melaniphy advises clients to "find sites along the peripheries," so that "you can control your own destiny" (Goodman 34).

15

So then, what is left? Perhaps the most obvious answer will suffice. When I was a waiter, and customers were dissatisfied with something, they did the most natural thing: they complained! That was all that was necessary. The moment a supervisor found out that there was a problem, he or she turned to solve that problem in an effort to maintain a good customer opinion. The same is true for Service America!

16

In an interview with Michael Loprete, director of Dining Services here at Wright State, I found that Service America is willing to listen to complaints. "I want comments," says Loprete, who is also a member of the Food Service Advisory Committee, an organization comprising several campus associations to investigate and resolve complaints about the food service. "We are here and accessible," he adds, "we are aware of problems and are attempting to address them . . . that is what the committees are for."

The Food Service Advisory Committee makes itself accessible by 17 electing representatives from many student organizations such as Student Government and Handicapped Services and by conducting interviews in the Woods, Hamilton Hall, and dining areas to collect student opinions. All complaints reach the Food Service Advisory Committee, which keeps the complaints on file. In addition, there are boxes available in every dining facility for student comments of either displeasure or praise. These boxes are locked, and only members of the Food Service Advisory Committee have the key.

The solution to the food service problem at Wright State lies in 18 the hands of the students. They have the power and the right to complain if they feel they are being, as one student so eloquently put it, "glued, screwed, and tattooed!" Instead of complaining to each other (which is quite often as far as many complaints go), students need to make their opinions known to Service America and the Food Service Advisory Committee. Service America's best incentive to do well is the renewal of its contract with WSU. If there is indeed large student dissatisfaction, then Service America's contract is threatened because the quality of the service it provides comes into question. Wright State is a good profitmaker for Service America, and it is an account they don't want to lose, so they will do what they can to keep public opinion high.

Individual complaints can best be handled by the managers of the 19 separate units. If you receive food that is cold or a bun that is hard and stale, ask to see the manager and resolve the problem then and there instead of carrying the problem back to your table and grumbling about it. If you receive rude and unfriendly service, or have a complaint that you feel cannot be resolved easily, leave a message in the comment box detailing your complaint, or contact your representative in the Food Service Advisory Committee.

Making your opinions known is the best way I know of to resolve 20 any problems that exist between the students and the food service. The students who make their opinions and complaints known will have them resolved in one manner or another, and by solving the students' problems as best they are able, Service America will ensure good public opinion and keep its contract. This arrangement is beneficial for both parties involved, and since my results concluded that there is no widespread discontent with the food service, there is no real justification for procedures any more radical than those I have suggested.

Perhaps a monopoly does exist at Wright State in the form of Ser- 21 vice America, but it is a monopoly that is ultimately controlled by its patrons, who have the freedom and the power to act on their opinions. The choice for action lies in their hands.

Works Cited

Goodman, Stephanie. "Dinner Is Served—At the Mall." *Adweek's Marketing Week* 24 July 1989: 30–34.

Loprete, Michael. Personal interview. 26 Feb. 1990.

CHAPTER 8

MAKING EVALUATIONS

*W*hile it's easy to make judgments, justifying them is another *matter. Rarely do we support our judgments with specific observations and evidence, and even more rarely do we make explicit the criteria by which we judge. In fact, evaluative criteria are often so deeply embedded in our worldview— understood by us so well—that it seems unnecessary to articulate them. As you read the three essays in this chapter, consider the criteria the writers use to make their judgments and how they establish those criteria, whether explicitly or implicitly.*

In "The Simpsons: A Mirror of Society," Ben McCorkle evaluates a television program that readers have undoubtedly heard about but perhaps not watched. Thus, he recalls memorable episodes and details from the program to provide a solid factual base for his evaluation, a move that enables him, as well, to persuade readers by using illustration that The Simpsons *is a satire. The criterion he reasons from in supporting* The Simpsons—*that satire creates "quality programming"—is, he believes, implicit and self-evident and, therefore, doesn't need articulation.*

Whether or not you're a fan of horror movies, Scott Hyder's opening narrative hook in "Poltergeist: It Knows What Scares You" will draw you into the world of horror. Like McCorkle, he provides imagery and plot synopsis to set up a shared base of evidence, then discusses the horror-movie genre more broadly to establish specific evaluative criteria. Hyder comparatively applies his criteria to other horror films before returning to Poltergeist *to argue how that film, in effect, "does it better." See if at the end you don't feel generally well informed about horror movies, a consequence due in part to the writer's thoroughly established evaluative criteria.*

In "Buzzworm: The Superior Magazine," Ilene Wolf backs up her evaluation of the environmental magazine Buzzworm *with solid detailed evidence, as well. Interestingly, her judgment relies on two kinds of criteria. The first is so commonly understood that she can simply describe the striking visual appeal of* Buzzworm *without stating explicitly that visual appeal is important for a magazine's success. The second, however, probably isn't so commonly understood. Since readers very likely don't know the technical features of magazine layout and design, Wolf spells them out as she applies them to argue* Buzzworm's *virtues.*

THE SIMPSONS:
A MIRROR OF SOCIETY

Ben McCorkle

■

Augusta College
Augusta, Georgia

I n recent years, a certain animated sitcom has caught the pub-   1
lic's attention, evoking reactions that are both favorable and unfavor-
able, but hardly ever apathetic. As a brilliant, socially aware satire, Matt
Groening's *The Simpsons* has effectively stirred different emotions from
different factions of the culturally deadened American populace, and for
this alone it should be recognized as "quality programming."

Often, *The Simpsons* is truly brutal parody, hurling barbs of hos-   2
tile commentary at our materialistic and gluttonous American lifestyle.
Many in the audience might be offended by this bullying, except that
it seems like harmless fun. For example, when father Homer Simpson
decides he would rather sleep in on a Sunday than attend church,
Groening is obviously pointing out a corruption of traditional values
within the family structure. But recognizing that people don't like to
be preached to, the show takes a comic approach, having God come to
talk to Homer, telling him to start his own religious sect. The hedo-
nism that Homer extols in the name of the Lord is both ludicrous and
hilariously funny, and viewers who might be offended are disarmed, so
that even the most conservative Republican grandmother is receptive
to the comic message.

Because it is a cartoon, some might scoff at *The Simpsons* and call   3
it a children's show. But this cartoon is clearly meant for a mass audience, including adults: it is shown during prime time rather than on Sat-

130

urday mornings, and, moreover, it appears on the Fox network, that paragon of broadcast debauchery. The cartoon format allows for visual freedom artistically and, because many people believe cartoons to be childish and incapable of making any real commentary on social values, may aid as well in the subtle presentation of the show's message.

The Simpson family has occasionally been described as a "nu-   4 clear" family, which obviously has a double meaning: first, the family consists of two parents and three children, and, second, Homer works at a nuclear power plant with very relaxed safety codes. The overused label *dysfunctional*, when applied to the Simpsons, suddenly takes on new meaning. Every episode seems to include a scene in which son Bart is being choked by his father, the baby is being neglected, or Homer sits in a drunken stupor transfixed by the television screen. The comedy in these scenes comes from the exaggeration of commonplace household events (although some talk shows and news programs would have us believe that these exaggerations are not confined to the madcap world of cartoons).

While Bart represents the mischievous demon-spawn and   5 Homer the dim-witted plow ox, the female characters serve as foils to counterbalance these male characters' unredeeming characteristics. Marge, the mother, is rational, considerate, and forgiving, always aware of her husband's shortcomings; younger sister Lisa is intelligent, well behaved, and an outstanding student; and baby Maggie is an innocent child. (Could the fact that the "good" members of the family all happen to be female reflect some feminist statement on Groening's part?)

It is said that "to err is human," in which case the Simpsons may   6 appear to be a little more human than the rest of us. They are constantly surrounded by their failures, yet seemingly unaware that their lives are often less than ideal. Their ability to accept the hand dealt them and endure without complaint is their most charming quality. Although not very bright as a whole, the Simpsons are survivors. Moreover, they exhibit a patriotic dedication to life, liberty, and the pursuit of happiness that should make every true American proud.

Ultimately, viewers find this family to be unwitting heroes, en-   7 during the incompetence and corruption of contemporary education, industry, government, religion, and, ironically, even television. Yet in spite of all the disheartening social problems it portrays, *The Simpsons* nevertheless remains funny. Whenever a scene threatens to turn melodramatic or raise an inescapably deep issue, the moment is saved by some piece of nonsense, often an absurdly gratuitous act of violence.

At a time when it seems that society is being destroyed by its own 8
designs, it is good to be able to hold up a mirror that shows us the extent of our problems. Neither escapist nor preachy, *The Simpsons* provides such a satiric mirror, a metaphoric reflection of our dissolving social foundation. More than that, *The Simpsons* is therapeutic: to be able
to laugh in the face of such problems is the ultimate catharsis.

POLTERGEIST:
IT KNOWS
WHAT SCARES YOU

Scott Hyder

■

University of Arizona
Tucson, Arizona

Y ou are an eight-year-old boy all tucked in for the night. Your 1
little sister is sleeping in the bed next to you. Suddenly, you hear a crash
of thunder, and through the window, you can see the big, old, growl-
ing tree in the lightning. It seems to be, well, to be making faces at you!
But, you are a big boy. Nothing scares *you*. Nothing at—BANG!
WHOOSH! The tree comes to life as it tumbles through the window,
grabbing you with its pulsating, hairy roots from your bed. As you
scream for Mommy, the closet door slowly opens and an invisible,
windlike presence kidnaps your sister. Your nice, cozy dreamhouse
turns into a living hell. Watch out! "They're hee-re!"

In June 1982, producer-director-writer Steven Spielberg defined 2
"horror" with a new word: *Poltergeist*. At first and final glance, *Poltergeist* is simply a riveting demonstration of a movie's power to terrify. It
creates honest thrills within the confines of a PG rating, reaching for
shock effects and the forced suspension of disbelief throughout the
movie. Spielberg wrote the story, coproduced it, and supervised the final
editing. The directing credit goes to Tobe Hooper, best known for his
cult shocker *The Texas Chainsaw Massacre*, which probably explains *Poltergeist*'s violence and slight crudeness.

Nevertheless, *Poltergeist* cannot be classified in the same horror 3
category with such movies as *A Nightmare on Elm Street*, where a de-
formed psychotic slashes his victims with razor-edged fingernails. Un-

like most horror flicks, *Poltergeist* works! Its success is due to excellent characters, music, and special effects—and to the fact that the story stays within the bounds of believability.

The movie takes place in a suburban housing tract. Steve (Craig   4
T. Nelson) and Diane (JoBeth Williams) Freeling have just purchased a new home when their adorable five-year-old daughter, Carole Anne (Heather O'Rourke), awakes to odd voices coming from the snowy TV screen that Steve falls asleep in front of during the late movie. She calls them the "TV people," and with the help of special-effects producer George Lucas and his Industrial Light and Magic, these people abduct little Carol Anne, provoking turbulence and misery for this once-happy family.

A mere synopsis simply cannot give a real feeling for the story. As   5
Steve Freeling says to the parapsychologists who have come to see the house, "You have to see it to believe it." Each character possesses a unique personality, which contributes to the overall feeling the audience has for the story. The characters are represented to be as normal and American as bologna sandwiches—Dad sells houses, Mom sings along to TV jingles. Spielberg likes these characters, illustrating their go-with-the-flow resilience. When things get suddenly hectic toward the climax, these people can display their fear and anger as well as summon their inner strengths. This is particularly evident when Tangina, the parapsychologist the Freelings hire, instructs Diane to lie to her daughter in order to lure Carol Anne into the light and save her.

"Tell her to go into the light," Tangina instructs. "Tell her that   6
you are in the light!"

"No," Diane replies with betrayed emotions.   7

Tangina immediately puts everything into the proper perspective.   8
"You can't choose between life and death when we're dealing with what's in between! Now tell her before it's too late!"

Such scenes clearly illustrate that Spielberg's characters are, in a   9
sense, the ordinary heroes of the movies.

A horror movie, however, cannot rely on terror, anger, and dis-   10
belief to hold its audience for two hours. Something needs to accompany these emotions, equally expressing the full extent of the characters' fear and anger. Music composer Jerry Goldsmith contributes his share of eeriness with his Academy Award–winning sound track. The basic theme is a lullaby (entitled "Carol Anne's Theme") that soothes the watcher, providing a cheerful, childlike innocence to the picture. The inverse is the ghost music that accompanies the abduction of Carol Anne and forces our stomachs to writhe. The music brings a straining,

vibrating tone that is responsible for 60 percent of the audience's terror. When the clown doll's hand wraps around Robbie's (Oliver Robbins) neck, the sudden blaring of Goldsmith's orchestra is what makes viewers swallow their stomachs. Without it, the scene would never slap our face or give our necks a backward whiplash. Goldsmith matches the actions and emotions of the characters with the corresponding instrumental music, enabling the audience to parallel their feelings with those delivered on the screen.

If a horror movie has a well-developed plot with superior actors 11 and an excellent score to accompany their emotions, then it should be a sure winner at the box office, right? Looking back at such movies as *Rosemary's Baby, The Exorcist,* and the original *Psycho,* one would obviously agree. *Poltergeist,* however, doesn't stop here. It goes even further by providing its audience with a special treat. With the help of *Star Wars* creator George Lucas, Spielberg and Hooper whip up a dazzling show of light and magic. There's an eerie parade of poltergeists in chiffons of light marching down the Freelings' staircase to the climactic scene as a huge, bright, nuclear-colored mouth strives to suck the Freeling children into their closet. Hooper's familiarity with film violence surfaces in a grotesque scene in which one of the parapsychologists hallucinates that he is tearing his face. Such shocking, hair-raising scenes as this make a huge contribution to horrifying the audience. Many horror films never achieve such reactions. *Poltergeist*'s precise timing with such effects makes it completely unpredictable as far as what is to come. From the first sign of a ghostlike hand jumping out of the TV to the staggering scene of dead bodies popping out of the half-dug swimming pool, the special-effects team draws every bit of energy out of the audience, dazzling them and forcing them to believe in the horror on the screen.

There have been many movies that possess superior ratings in all 12 of the above. Such movies as John Carpenter's *The Thing* and David Croneberg's *Scanners* won raves for superior acting, background music, and special effects. Why was *Poltergeist* accepted at the box office more than other such movies? Every movie is forced to set up boundaries of believability through certain actions and concepts, and at one point these boundaries will be accepted by the viewer. In *Indiana Jones and the Temple of Doom,* Spielberg distinguished boundaries within which Indiana Jones defined his heroic stunts. Spielberg, however, unfortunately crossed his boundaries during a scene in which Indiana Jones jumps from one track to another with a moving train cart. From previous observations of Indiana Jones's capabilities, the audience is unable to accept this, nodding their heads with a "give me a break" expression.

In *Poltergeist*, Spielberg and Hooper remain within their established boundaries. Unlike most horror movies that have unfeasible killers who are incapable of dying or monsters that pop out of people's stomachs, *Poltergeist* focuses on the supernatural—a subject with *very wide* boundaries. Because of our lack of knowledge in the area, we are "at the mercy of the writers and directors," as Alfred Hitchcock has phrased it. The boundaries can be greater than most horror movies because of *Poltergeist*'s subject matter. The characters' disbelief of their surroundings encourages the audience to accept what is in front of them. Hence, *Poltergeist* successfully stays within its limits, taking them to their maximum, but luring the audience to believe the characters' situation. 13

Poltergeist reflects a lot of the fears that most of us grow up with: seeing scary shadows from the light in your closet, making sure your feet are not dangling over the bed, forming scary images of the objects in your room. As Spielberg's *E.T.* reminisces about our childhood dreams, *Poltergeist* surfaces our childhood nightmares. With its characters, music, and special effects, and its clearly distinguished boundaries of belief, *Poltergeist* is able to capture its audience with its unique thrills, allowing viewers to link their most inner-locked fears to those on the screen. *Poltergeist:* It knows what scares you! 14

BUZZWORM:
THE SUPERIOR
MAGAZINE

Ilene Wolf

■

University of California, San Diego
La Jolla, California

Many people today exist within their environment without   1
really knowing anything about it. If this ignorance continues, we will
undoubtedly destroy the world in which we live. Only by gaining a better understanding of our planet will we be able to preserve our fragile
environment from pollution, hazardous waste, endangerment of species,
and ravaging of the land. A new magazine is dedicated to enlightening
the general public about these important issues. It is called *Buzzworm*.

What makes *Buzzworm* superior to other magazines dealing with   2
the same subject is that it not only fully explores all of the aspects of the
environment but it does so in an objective manner. *Buzzworm* effectively
tackles the controversial question of how best to protect our planet and
conveys the information in a way that all audiences can understand. In
fact, the term *buzzworm*, borrowed from the Old West, refers to a rattlesnake. The rattlesnake represents an effective form of communication, for when it rattles or buzzes it causes an immediate reaction in
those who are near. Thus the purpose of *Buzzworm* is to create a reaction in its readers regarding the conservation and preservation of the
environment.

One of *Buzzworm*'s most striking features is its visual appeal. Ex-   3
cellent photographs complement the articles. Contrasted with the pho-
tography in *Sierra*, another environmental magazine, the superb photographs in *Buzzworm* only seem more striking. The summer 1989

137

issue of *Buzzworm* features a dramatic, full-page color picture of the gray wolf, which catches the reader's eye and draws attention to the article concerning the endangerment of the gray wolf's habitat. An issue of *Sierra* from the same year also has a picture of the gray wolf, yet it is not only smaller but the colors are not as clear—resulting in a less effective picture. Whereas both photographs of the animal pertain to their corresponding articles, it is the one in *Buzzworm* that makes the reader stop and discover the plight of the gray wolf.

Not only must a photograph be of excellent quality but it also must be placed correctly in the layout to enhance the article. The reader should be able to look at the picture and receive some information about the article it corresponds to. *Buzzworm*'s pictures of the East African Masai convey specific information about the tribe. Startling photographs depict the Masai in their traditional dress, focusing on the elaborate beadwork done by the women and the exquisite headdresses worn by the warriors. Looking at one picture of a young warrior wearing a lion's mane headdress, the reader gets a sense of the importance of the ritual and of the great respect that is earned by becoming a warrior. Another picture depicts a mother intently watching her daughter as she learns the art of beading. The look on the woman's face displays the care that goes into the beadwork, which has been an important part of their heritage for many generations. Thus, even before reading the article about the Masai, readers have some understanding of the Masai culture and traditions.

Another functional and informative aspect of *Buzzworm*'s layout is the use of subfeatures within an article. A subfeature functions in two ways, first by breaking up the monotony of a solid page of print, and second by giving the curious reader additional information. An article entitled "Double Jeopardy," for example, gives the reader an option of learning more about the subject through two subfeatures. The article itself describes the detrimental effects that excessive whale watching and research are believed to have on the humpback whale. To find further information about what might be contributing to the already low numbers of the humpback whale, one can read the subfeature, "Humpback Whale Survival." Furthermore, for the reader who is not familiar with the subject, there is a second subfeature, entitled "Natural History," which gives general information about the humpback whale. No such subfeatures can be found anywhere in *Sierra*.

In addition to being an effective way of adding pertinent information to the article, the subfeatures also add to the unity of the magazine. The subfeatures in *Buzzworm* all share a common gray background color, adding to the continuity in layout from one article to the next. This produces a cleaner, more finished, and visually appealing magazine.

Once again, *Buzzworm* shows superior layout design in keeping   7
the articles from being overrun by advertisements. I realize that ads do generate necessary revenue for the magazine, but nothing is more annoying than an article constantly interrupted by ads. *Buzzworm*'s few ads are all in the back of the magazine. In fact, not once does an ad interrupt an article. On the other hand, *Sierra* is filled with advertisements that are allowed to interrupt articles, which only frustrates the reader and detracts from the articles.

Buzzworm is unique in that it focuses on more than just one aspect of the environment. In contrast, *Sierra* devoted its entire September/October 1989 issue to one subject, the preservation of the public lands in the United States. Although it is a topic worthy of such discussion, readers prefer more variety to choose from. The content of *Buzzworm* ranges from the humpback whale to the culture of the Masai to a profile of three leading conservationists. The great variety of issues covered in *Buzzworm* makes it more likely to keep the reader's attention than *Sierra*.

Buzzworm's ability to inform the reader is not limited to the in-   9
formation in its articles. Captions also play a large part. Readers who are too lazy to read an entire article most often will look at the pictures and read the captions. Thus *Buzzworm*'s long and detailed captions are like miniature paragraphs, giving out more details than the terse captions in *Sierra*, which usually consist of only a few words. The difference in the amount of information in the two magazines is obvious from a look at a typical caption in *Buzzworm*: "Finding relaxation of a different kind, Earthwatch participants spend a vacation patrolling beaches and assisting female turtles in finding a secluded nesting area" compared to one in *Sierra*, "Joshua tree with Clark Mountain in background." Both captions give a description of their corresponding pictures, but only the caption found in *Buzzworm* gives any indication of what the article is about. The captions in *Buzzworm* supplement the articles, whereas the captions in *Sierra* only give brief descriptions of the pictures.

Finally, *Buzzworm* is objective, a rare quality in environmental   10
magazines. An article on tourism versus environmental responsibility focuses on both the environmental and economic aspects of tourism, stating that while tourism generates income, it often destroys places of natural beauty that are so often visited. In contrast to this point of view,

the article also cites examples where tourism has actually helped to preserve the environment. For every argument presented in *Buzzworm*, the counterargument is also presented. This balance is important, for readers must have all of the facts to be able to make well-informed judgments about controversial issues.

Despite all of its wonderful aspects, *Buzzworm* does have its flaws. 11 Some of its graphics pale next to the color photographs. Also, the photograph sizes should be varied more in size to create a visually more appealing layout. Except for these minor flaws, *Buzzworm* achieves its goal of appealing to its readers. In informing the general public about conservation and protection of our environment, *Buzzworm* is far more effective than *Sierra*.

CHAPTER 9

SPECULATING ABOUT CAUSES

*I*t's always a challenge to look squarely and see beyond the obvious *features of things. Close examination in an essay that reveals not-so-obvious, even hidden, dimensions of an issue frees the writer and the reader to explore and discover fresh paths to understanding. A common thread in the four essays in this chapter is their concern with such discovery, reflected in the way each is so thoroughly researched and documented. This fact should raise an important question: Do speculative essays need to be researched and documented? You might consider the question "speculatively" and ask: What causes an effective speculative essay? As you read each one (your "initial research" into the question), think about how its authority would be affected by the absence of documentation. Indeed, what are the causes of authority?*

Reese Mason opens "Basketball and the Urban Poor" with an urgency that situates the phenomenon he writes about: poor urban athletes risking their lives for sports. Because college athletics are so prominent in our society, Mason doesn't need to convince readers that the phenomenon exists. By describing the death of college basketball star Hank Gathers, he uses the specific incident to hook readers into the broader phenomenon he wishes to explore. Mason serves up one remote causal connection—that the American dream is the motivating force—but keeps his analysis close to the immediate causes of money, popularity, and education.

Chloë Elizabeth Arnold cites Census Bureau statistics to establish the trend she writes about. Her analysis relies on specific evidence and reasoning to confirm the plausibility of the four immediate causes that she proposes to explain recent trends in childbearing. At the end of the essay, Arnold moves into broader speculation about more remote, background causes and discusses the influence that pervasive social attitudes toward women have had.

In "What Makes a Serial Killer?" La Donna Beaty proposes a range of causes for this unsettling social problem. Instead of a simplistic answer, she makes clear the multidimensional nature of the phenomenon and its causes. In the end, Beaty's essay uncovers, perhaps unknowingly, the value of speculative writing itself: when simple answers can't be "proved," it helps to think reasonably through the possibilities and put the best proposal forward.

In her essay, "The Rise in Reported Incidents of Sexual Harassment," Sarah West opens with a brief history of increased sexual-harassment reports between 1964 and 1994. She then asks the question: why such a big increase in such a short period of time? By citing source materials that range from daily newspapers to specialized journals, West reasons about speculations that might explain the causes, structuring her essay around three possibilities: corporate willingness to take responsibility for educating their employees; media exposure of high-profile cases that raise public consciousness of sexual harassment; and, finally, the greater percentage of women in the workplace. Note how West critically analyzes and weighs the plausibility of each possibility.

BASKETBALL AND THE URBAN POOR

Reese Mason

■

University of California, Riverside
Riverside, California

For a while there, Gathers had beaten the system, the cycle that traps so many black youths in frustration and poverty.

Art Spander

On the evening of March 4, 1990, much like any other night, I sat in my living room fixed to the television as ESPN's Sport Center broadcast the day's sporting news. The lead story was about the 1989 national leader in rebounding and scoring in collegiate basketball, Loyola Marymount's Hank Gathers. It was not unusual for Gathers to be in the news, given his many fantastic performances and displays of great character. He had become much more than a premier basketball player since achieving athletic stardom. Yes, Hank Gathers had become an inspiration to all those who, like himself, had the misfortune of being born poor. This story, however, was not about a new scoring record, or a buzzer-beating shot. Nor was it a commentary on how Gathers had not forgotten what community he hailed from, and how he intended to move his mother and son out of poverty when he made it to the "Show" (Almond). This news story was about a twenty-three-year-old basketball player collapsing and dying on the court.

In utter dismay, I immediately demanded some reason for the unbelievable events. After an incident some three months earlier, Gathers had been tested and found to have cardiomyopathy (a type of ar-

1

2

rhythmia). How in the world could the doctors have allowed him to continue playing? With such a heart defect, how could he allow himself to continue playing? How could the game of basketball have become more important to Hank Gathers than life itself? The night of March 4 was a sleepless one for this sports fan. I lay awake in restless wonder at what could have compelled a man of my age to risk his life for a game.

The answers came to me the next day in a follow-up story about   3
the tragic death. The piece was a tribute to the life of Hank Gathers. Appropriately, the story began where Gathers's life began, and suddenly, with one shot of the camera, I understood. I understood what drove him to greatness on the basketball court. I understood what compelled Gathers to continue playing even after he knew he had a heart defect. Like most middle-class sports fanatics, I was well aware that many African American athletes come from the inner city. I was even aware that Gathers had risen out of a Philadelphia ghetto to achieve greatness in college basketball. Never, though, had I really sat down and considered why growing up in the ghetto might make the game of basketball seem so important—and, in Gathers's case, as valuable as life itself.

Basketball is popular among the urban poor because it is virtually   4
the only way for young African American men to make it, to become idolized superstars. Unlike football or baseball, basketball requires little money or formal organization to play. All that is needed is a few dollars for a ball and access to a hoop, found at any school or playground. Additionally, it can be practiced and all but perfected without the need for coaches, expensive facilities, or even many other players.

The examples of basketball stars like Magic Johnson and Michael   5
Jordan probably inspired Gathers, as they have thousands of others who cling to the game of basketball as their ticket out of the ghetto. There aren't many alternatives. The unemployment rate for African American teenagers is over 40 percent, and what work they can find is mostly low-paying, dead-end jobs. Many inner-city youth resort to drugs and crime, and not surprisingly, about a quarter of all African American men between twenty and twenty-nine wind up in jail, on parole, or on probation (*Statistical Abstract*).

Our society offers those who can play basketball well an educa-   6
tion that might not otherwise be obtained. Education is a limited and insufficient resource to the urban poor. There are no easy answers, I admit, but the facts are indisputable. In order to get a quality education, the poor have to win scholarships. Because of its popularity in the United States, and its college connection, basketball has become one

144

avenue to a higher education. Even when college basketball players are unable to continue playing in the pros, their university degrees may lead to other good jobs and thus to economic success.

Yet, education is not the motivating factor behind the success stories of the poor any more than it is among the success stories of the middle class; money is. After all, money is what you are judged on here in the United States, along with popular recognition. Basketball provides an avenue from the urban ghetto to the highest echelons in the United States via money and popularity. Gathers was honest about what was important to him when he said, "I'm in college to play basketball. The degree is important to me, but not that important" (Hudson and Almond). Gathers understood that basketball was the vehicle that would take him where he wanted to go. It offered him money (multimillions, in fact), education, and popularity — the three components of the American dream.

We recognize Hank Gathers because of his tragic death, but only because he was a fantastic basketball player. It is hard for us to admit, but who would have taken time out for Gathers and his family had he died of a heart defect while playing ball in the Rowand Rosen housing project where his family still lives? Those who were close to him, assuredly, but not the nation. This is why basketball was so important to Gathers, and it may be why he continued playing despite the risk of dying on the court. Hank Gathers's story helps us to see why basketball is so popular among, and dominated by, the urban poor. Basketball is an E-Ticket out of the ghetto, one of the best available means of getting nationwide recognition and providing for their family.

Works Cited

Almond, Elliot. "Gathers, Pepperdine's Lewis Had Special Bond." *Los Angeles Times* 7 Mar. 1990: C8.

Hudson, Maryann, and Elliot Almond. "Gathers Suit Asks for $32.5 Million." *Los Angeles Times* 21 Apr. 1990: C1, C20.

Spander, Art. "Who's to Blame for Gathers' Tragic Death?" *Sporting News* 19 Mar. 1990: 5.

Statistical Abstract of the United States 1989. U.S. Bureau of Census, 109th ed. Washington: GPO, 1989.

A Trend in Childbearing

Chloë Elizabeth Arnold

■

University of California, San Diego
La Jolla, California

Open your eyes! Look around and notice the mothers with   1
newborns and wrinkles, the pregnant women with gray hair. Do you
remember seeing so many older mothers twenty years ago? Probably
not. These women reflect an increasing trend: upper-middle-class
women having children much, much later than their mothers ever did.
According to a 1989 Census Bureau survey, more than half of the
women aged thirty to thirty-four who do not have any children still in-
tend to have a family (Kasindorf 24). The 1990 Census Bureau survey
revealed that "the number of women thirty-five and older giving birth
for the first time has quadrupled in the past decade" (Roan 10). However, these statistics do not apply to all women within the United States.
Other studies suggest that the trend is a predominately upper-middle-
class phenomenon (Coady 62), and researchers have found that "delayed
childbearing is less prevalent among black women than among nonblack
women" (Bloom and Trussell 591). While there are probably as many
reasons for later childbearing as there are individual women, a few
common causes contribute to the decision.

Perhaps the most obvious and basic explanation is simply the im-   2
mense advancement in medical technology. While women could always
become pregnant until about the age of forty, doctors even ten years
ago strongly advised against later pregnancies because of the increased
risks for both mother and child. Today, however, amniocentesis tests

for pregnant women over the age of thirty are standard procedure. By developing some of the cells that float around in the amniotic fluid of the uterus, doctors can determine whether the child suffers from any genetic abnormalities. Another prenatal test, called chorionic villi sampling, has recently been developed, and "its advantage over amniocentesis is that it can be performed as early as the ninth week of pregnancy ... [while] amniocentesis is not usually done until the sixteenth or eighteenth week" (Kasindorf 26). Such tests make pregnancies in older women much safer. In addition, middle-aged women experiencing problems conceiving or maintaining pregnancy can now participate in experimental research involving "the use of donor eggs and embryo transfer" in place of traditional in vitro fertilization (Roan 10). The most radical of such new medical technology enables post-menopausal women "to bear children successfully [by receiving] an embryo from donor eggs and hormone injections in the first three months of pregnancy" (Roan 10). These advances in obstetrical and gynecological medicine benefit both older women with fertility problems and women who are already pregnant.

Another medically based explanation for later childbearing is advances in birth control. Up until about thirty years ago, the basic choices were condoms, the rhythm method, coitus interruptus, and diaphragms. But with the introduction of oral contraceptives in the early 1960s, women gained greater control over their reproductive capabilities. Today, improved methods of birth control are constantly being developed and tested. (The "abortion pill" and RU 486, for example, are currently available in Europe and soon may be in the United States.) As it has become increasingly convenient and socially acceptable to use some effective form of birth control, women have been better able to control the decision as to when to have children, allowing them more easily to delay starting a family.

Another cause of delayed childbirth is economic. Increasingly, women are choosing to live on their own, and they are also marrying later in life. In 1860, the mean age at first marriage was 20.8 years, and by 1960 that number was still only 21.0; but in 1980, the average age at first marriage was 24.0 years (Anderton 49; Menken 476). Most single-income, single women in their twenties do not have the time or financial resources to raise a child by themselves *and* work, and so are unlikely to bear children until later in life.

Even young married women are more likely now to find it necessary to work as the single-income household becomes increasingly rare due to the higher cost of living and generally lower wages. Rather than raising a child in day care, many such women are delaying child-bearing, as well. During the early 1960s, first births typically occurred fourteen months after marriage, yet eighteen years later the interval had increased to twenty-four months (Coady 1). Moreover, researchers are currently finding that "a longer first birth interval may promote marital stability by giving the couple time to adjust to marriage . . . and acquire the finances necessary to raise a child . . . thus [reducing] marital strain that is brought on by economic pressure" (Wineberg 92).

While finances force some women to work and thus delay starting a family, many others choose to pursue careers and personal interests before even considering having children. One authority discovered that 64 percent of the women in her sample survey "intentionally delayed childbearing in order to reach specific goals" such as finishing college and establishing their careers (Coady 65). 6

Clearly, an increase in the number of working women is an immediate cause of delayed childbearing. But why are more women working? I believe that a close interrelationship exists among the causes of the trend. Many of the reasons for delayed childbearing result from the equal rights movement that began in the early 1960s. Particularly for women who grew up in the 1960s and are now middle-aged, the equal rights movement spelled not just equality but also freedoms their mothers did not enjoy: the freedom to decide for themselves what they wanted from life and the freedom to act on it, the freedom to control their own bodies through the use of birth control, and the freedom to enter the workforce as something other than nurses, teachers, or secretaries. Women discovered new options and no longer felt required to define themselves by having a family. Traditionally, young women got married straight out of high school and then stayed at home to be good wives, mothers, and housekeepers. Those who did attend college frequently "met a nice boy" and then dropped out to become "his wife." However, young women who grew up during the 1950s and 1960s were given other options. They were encouraged to achieve and make something of themselves as individuals; as a group, they generally had higher educational expectations than the generation before them. A national fertility study concluded that "educational attainment had a sizeable delaying effect on age [of the mother] at first birth" (Marini 492). Thus, because they remained in school longer, this generation of women frequently delayed marriage and pursued careers and other personal goals. Many have only within the last decade considered starting a family. 7

The greater variety and acceptance of birth control, the current 8 economic situation, and the multiple changes brought about by the equal rights movement of the 1960s and the 1970s have led many women to delay childbearing until their thirties and beyond. And with continuing advances in medical technology, there may be no end to the trend of delayed childbearing among white, upper-middle-class women. As one scientist says, "Some researchers now refuse to put an age limit on motherhood" (Roan 10).

Works Cited

Anderton, Douglas L. "Urbanization, Secularization, and Birth Spacing: A Case Study of an Historical Fertility Transition." *Sociological Quarterly* 27 (Spring 1986): 43–62.

Bloom, David E., and James Trussell. "What Are the Determinants of Delayed Childbearing and Permanent Childlessness in the United States?" *Demography* 21 (1984): 591–611.

Coady, Susan Stickel. "Delayed Childbearing: Correlates of Maternal Satisfaction at One Year Postpartum." Diss. Ohio S U, 1982.

Kasindorf, J. "Mommy Oldest: Having Babies at 45 and Beyond." *New York* 17 July 1989: 22–29.

Marini, Margaret Mooney. "Women's Educational Attainment and the Timing of Entry into Parenthood." *American Sociological Review* 49 (1984): 491–511.

Menken, Jane. "Age and Fertility: How Late Can You Wait?" *Demography* 22 (1985): 469–83.

Roan, Shari. "Giving Birth to a Controversy." *Los Angeles Times* 30 Oct. 1990: 1+.

Wineberg, Howard. "Duration between Marriage and First Birth and Marital Instability." *Social Biology* 35 (Spring/Summer 1988): 91–102.

WHAT MAKES
A SERIAL KILLER?

La Donna Beaty

■

Sinclair Community College
Dayton, Ohio

Jeffrey Dahmer, John Wayne Gacy, Mark Allen Smith, Richard 1
Chase, Ted Bundy—the list goes on and on. These five men alone have
been responsible for at least ninety deaths, and many suspect that their
victims may total twice that number. They are serial killers, the most
feared and hated of criminals. What deep, hidden secret makes them
lust for blood? What can possibly motivate a person to kill over and over
again with no guilt, no remorse, no hint of human compassion? What
makes a serial killer?

Serial killings are not a new phenomenon. In 1798, for example, 2
Micajah and Wiley Harpe traveled the backwoods of Kentucky and
Tennessee in a violent, year-long killing spree that left at least twenty—
and possibly as many as thirty-eight—men, women, and children dead.
Their crimes were especially chilling as they seemed particularly to
enjoy grabbing small children by the ankles and smashing their heads
against trees (Holmes and DeBurger 28). In modern society, however,
serial killings have grown to near epidemic proportions. Ann Rule, a
respected author and expert on serial murders, stated in a seminar at
the University of Louisville on serial murder that between 3,500 and
5,000 people become victims of serial murder each year in the United
States alone (qtd. in Holmes and DeBurger 21). Many others estimate
that there are close to 350 serial killers currently at large in our society
(Holmes and DeBurger 22).

Fascination with murder and murderers is not new, but researchers in recent years have made great strides in determining the characteristics of criminals. Looking back, we can see how naive early experts were in their evaluations: in 1911, for example, Italian criminologist Cesare Lombrosco concluded that "murderers as a group [are] biologically degenerate [with] bloodshot eyes, aquiline noses, curly black hair, strong jaws, big ears, thin lips, and menacing grins" (qtd. in Lunde 84). Today, however, we don't expect killers to have fangs that drip human blood, and many realize that the boy-next-door may be doing more than woodworking in his basement. While there are no specific physical characteristics shared by all serial killers, they are almost always male and 92 percent are white. Most are between the ages of twenty-five and thirty-five and often physically attractive. While they may hold a job, many switch employment frequently as they become easily frustrated when advancement does not come as quickly as expected. They tend to believe that they are entitled to whatever they desire but feel that they should have to exert no effort to attain their goals (Samenow 88, 96). What could possibly turn attractive, ambitious human beings into cold-blooded monsters?

One popular theory suggests that many murderers are the product of our violent society. Our culture tends to approve of violence and find it acceptable, even preferable, in many circumstances (Holmes and DeBurger 27). According to research done in 1970, one out of every four men and one out of every six women believed that it was appropriate for a husband to hit his wife under certain conditions (Holmes and DeBurger 33). This emphasis on violence is especially prevalent in television programs. Violence occurs in 80 percent of all prime-time shows, while cartoons, presumably made for children, average eighteen violent acts per hour. It is estimated that by the age of eighteen, the average child will have viewed more than 16,000 television murders (Holmes and DeBurger 34). Some experts feel that children demonstrate increasingly aggressive behavior with each violent act they view (Lunde 15) and become so accustomed to violence that these acts seem normal (Lunde 35). In fact, most serial killers do begin to show patterns of aggressive behavior at a young age. It is, therefore, possible that after viewing increasing amounts of violence, such children determine that this is acceptable behavior; when they are then punished for similar actions, they may become confused and angry and eventually lash out by committing horrible, violent acts.

Another theory concentrates on the family atmosphere into which the serial killer is born. Most killers state that they experienced psychological abuse as children and never established good relationships with the male figures in their lives (Ressler, Burgess, and Douglas 19). As children, they were often rejected by their parents and received little nurturing (Lunde 94; Holmes and DeBurger 64–70). It has also been established that the families of serial killers often move repeatedly, never allowing the child to feel a sense of stability; in many cases, they are also forced to live outside the family home before reaching the age of eighteen (Ressler, Burgess, and Douglas 19–20). Our culture's tolerance for violence may overlap with such family dynamics: with 79 percent of the population believing that slapping a twelve-year-old is either necessary, normal, or good, it is no wonder that serial killers relate tales of physical abuse (Holmes and DeBurger 30; Ressler, Burgess, and Douglas 19–20) and view themselves as the "black sheep" of the family. They may even, perhaps unconsciously, assume this same role in society.

While the foregoing analysis portrays the serial killer as a lost, 6 lonely, abused, little child, another theory, based on the same information, gives an entirely different view. In this analysis, the killer is indeed rejected by his family but only after being repeatedly defiant, sneaky, and threatening. As verbal lies and destructiveness increase, the parents give the child the distance he seems to want in order to maintain a small amount of domestic peace (Samenow 13). This interpretation suggests that the killer shapes his parents much more than his parents shape him. It also denies that the media can influence a child's mind and turn him into something that he doesn't already long to be. Since most children view similar amounts of violence, the argument goes, a responsible child filters what he sees and will not resort to criminal activity no matter how acceptable it seems to be (Samenow 15–18). In 1930, the noted psychologist Alfred Adler seemed to find this true of any criminal. As he put it, "With criminals it is different: they have a private logic, a private intelligence. They are suffering from a wrong outlook upon the world, a wrong estimate of their own importance and the importance of other people" (qtd. in Samenow 20).

Most people agree that Jeffrey Dahmer or Ted Bundy had to be 7 "crazy" to commit horrendous multiple murders, and scientists have long maintained that serial killers are indeed mentally disturbed (Lunde 48). While the percentage of murders committed by mental hospital patients is much lower than that among the general population (Lunde 35), it cannot be ignored that the rise in serial killings happened at almost the same time as the deinstitutionalization movement in the mental health–care system during the 1960s (Markman and Bosco 266).

While reform was greatly needed in the mental health–care system, it has now become nearly impossible to hospitalize those with severe problems. In the United States, people have a constitutional right to remain mentally ill. Involuntary commitment can only be accomplished if the person is deemed dangerous to self, dangerous to others, or gravely disabled. However, in the words of Ronald Markman, "According to the way that the law is interpreted, if you can go to the mailbox to pick up your social security check, you're not gravely disabled even if you think you're living on Mars"; even if a patient is thought to be dangerous, he or she cannot be held longer than ninety days unless it can be proved that the patient actually committed dangerous acts while in the hospital (Markman and Bosco 267). Many of the most heinous criminals have had long histories of mental illness but could not be hospitalized due to these stringent requirements. Richard Chase, the notorious Vampire of Sacramento, believed that he needed blood in order to survive, and while in the care of a psychiatric hospital, he often killed birds and other small animals in order to quench this desire. When he was released, he went on to kill eight people, one of them an eighteen-month-old baby (Biondi and Hecox 206). Edmund Kemper was equally insane. At the age of fifteen, he killed both of his grandparents and spent five years in a psychiatric facility. Doctors determined that he was "cured" and released him into an unsuspecting society. He killed eight women, including his own mother (Lunde 53–56). The world was soon to be disturbed by a cataclysmic earthquake, and Herbert Mullin knew that he had been appointed by God to prevent the catastrophe. The fervor of his religious delusion resulted in a death toll of thirteen (Lunde 63–81). All of these men had been treated for their mental disorders, and all were released by doctors who did not have enough proof to hold them against their will.

Recently, studies have given increasing consideration to the genetic makeup of serial killers. The connection between biology and behavior is strengthened by research in which scientists have been able to develop a violently aggressive strain of mice simply through selective inbreeding (Taylor 23). These studies have caused scientists to become increasingly interested in the limbic system of the brain, which houses the amygdala, an almond-shaped structure located in the front of the temporal lobe. It has long been known that surgically altering that portion of the brain, in an operation known as a lobotomy, is one way of controlling behavior. This surgery was used frequently in the 1960s but has since been discontinued as it also erases most of a person's personality. More recent developments, however, have shown that temporal

8

lobe epilepsy causes electrical impulses to be discharged directly into the amygdala. When this electronic stimulation is re-created in the laboratory, it causes violent behavior in lab animals. Additionally, other forms of epilepsy do not cause abnormalities in behavior, except during seizure activity. Temporal lobe epilepsy is linked with a wide range of antisocial behavior, including anger, paranoia, and aggression. It is also interesting to note that this form of epilepsy produces extremely unusual brain waves. These waves have been found in only 10 to 15 percent of the general population, but over 79 percent of known serial killers test positive for these waves (Taylor 28–33).

The look at biological factors that control human behavior is by no means limited to brain waves or other brain abnormalities. Much work is also being done with neurotransmitters, levels of testosterone, and patterns of trace minerals. While none of these studies are conclusive, they all show a high correlation between antisocial behavior and chemical interactions within the body (Taylor 63–69).   9

One of the most common traits that all researchers have noted among serial killers is heavy use of alcohol. Whether this correlation is brought about by external factors or whether alcohol is an actual stimulus that causes certain behavior is still unclear, but the idea deserves consideration. Lunde found that the majority of those who commit murder had been drinking beforehand and commonly had a urine alcohol level of between .20 and .29, nearly twice the legal level of intoxication (31–32). Additionally, 70 percent of the families that reared serial killers had verifiable records of alcohol abuse (Ressler, Burgess, and Douglas 17). Jeffrey Dahmer had been arrested in 1981 on charges of drunkenness and, before his release from prison on sexual assault charges, his father had written a heartbreaking letter which pleaded that Jeffrey be forced to undergo treatment for alcoholism, a plea that, if heeded, might have changed the course of future events (Davis 70, 103). Whether alcoholism is a learned behavior or an inherited predisposition is still hotly debated, but a 1979 report issued by Harvard Medical School stated that "[a]lcoholism in the biological parent appears to be a more reliable predictor of alcoholism in the children than any other environmental factor examined" (qtd. in Taylor 117). While alcohol was once thought to alleviate anxiety and depression, we now know that it can aggravate and intensify such moods (Taylor 110), which may lead to irrational feelings of powerlessness that are brought under control only when the killer proves he has the ultimate power to control life and death.   10

"Man's inhumanity to man" began when Cain killed Abel, but this   11 legacy has grown to frightening proportions, as evidenced by the vast number of books that line the shelves of modern bookstores—row after row of titles dealing with death, anger, and blood. We may never know what causes a serial killer to exact his revenge on an unsuspecting society. But we need to continue to probe the interior of the human brain to discover the delicate balance of chemicals that controls behavior. We need to be able to fix what goes wrong. We must also work harder to protect our children. Their cries must not go unheard. Their pain must not become so intense that it demands bloody revenge. As today becomes tomorrow, we must remember the words of Ted Bundy, one of the most ruthless serial killers of our time: "Most serial killers are people who kill for the pure pleasure of killing and cannot be rehabilitated. Some of the killers themselves would even say so" (qtd. in Holmes and DeBurger 150).

Works Cited

Biondi, Ray, and Walt Hecox. *The Dracula Killer.* New York: Simon, 1992.

Davis, Ron. *The Milwaukee Murders.* New York: St. Martin's, 1991.

Holmes, Ronald M., and James DeBurger. *Serial Murder.* Newbury Park, CA: Sage, 1988.

Lunde, Donald T. *Murder and Madness.* San Francisco: San Francisco Book, 1976.

Markman, Ronald, and Dominick Bosco. *Alone with the Devil.* New York: Doubleday, 1989.

Ressler, Robert K., Ann W. Burgess, and John E. Douglas. *Sexual Homicide— Patterns and Motives.* Lexington, MA: Heath, 1988.

Samenow, Stanton E. *Inside the Criminal Mind.* New York: Times, 1984.

Taylor, Lawrence. *Born to Crime.* Westport, CT: Greenwood, 1984.

THE RISE IN REPORTED INCIDENTS OF SEXUAL HARASSMENT

Sarah West

•

University of Houston
Houston, Texas

To those students who recently graduated from high school, 1
it sounds like the Dark Ages, but it wasn't. It was only thirty years ago.
Until 1964, an employee who refused to give in to his or her employer's
sexual advances could be fired—legally. An employee being constantly
humiliated by a coworker could be forced either to deal with the lewd
comments, the stares, and the touching or to just quit his or her job. It
is strange to think that sexual harassment was perfectly legal in the
United States until Congress passed the Civil Rights Act of 1964.

But even after 1964, sexual harassment still persisted. It was not 2
commonly known exactly what sexual harassment was or that federal
laws against it existed. Often when an employee was sexually harassed
on the job, he or she felt too alienated and humiliated to speak out
against it (Martell and Sullivan 6). During the 1970s and 1980s, however, sexual-harassment victims began coming forth to bring justice to
their harassers, albeit very slowly. Then suddenly in the 1990s, the
number of sexual-harassment complaints and lawsuits sharply rose. According to a 1994 survey conducted by the Society for Human Resource Management, the percentage of human-resource professionals
who have reported that their departments handled at least one sexual-
harassment complaint rose from 35 percent in 1991 to 65 percent in
1994. Why did this large increase occur in such a short amount of time?

One significant reason for the rise in reported incidents of sexual 3 harassment may be the increased awareness of what constitutes sexual harassment. There are two distinct types of sexual harassment, and although their formal names may be unfamiliar, the situations they describe will most certainly ring a bell. *Hostile environment* sexual harassment occurs when a supervisor, coworker, or classmate gives the victim "unwelcome sexual attention" that "interferes with (his or her) ability to work or creates an intimidating or offensive atmosphere" (Stanko and Werner 15). *Quid pro quo* sexual harassment occurs when "a workplace superior demands some degree of sexual favor" and either threatens to or does retaliate in a way that "has a tangible effect on the working conditions of the harassment victim" if he or she refuses to comply (Stanko and Werner 15).

Companies and corporations are largely responsible for the rise in awareness concerning sexual harassment. After the passage of the Civil Rights Act of 1991, which allowed, among other things, larger damage awards for sexually harassed employees, thus increasing employers' liability in sexual-harassment cases, many employers began to take a new look at sexual harassment in the workplace. Suddenly, it became possible for a company to lose millions in a single sexual-harassment case. For example, Rena Weeks, a legal secretary in San Francisco, sued the law firm of Baker & McKenzie for $3.5 million after their employee Martin Greenstein "dumped candy down the breast pocket of her blouse, groped her, pressed her from behind and pulled her arms back to 'see which one (breast) is bigger' " ("Workplace"). The jury awarded Weeks $7.1 million in punitive damages, twice what she sought in her lawsuit ("Workplace"). 4

In addition, it has been acknowledged that the mere existence of sexual harassment in a company can lead to "hidden costs" such as absenteeism, lower productivity, and loss of valuable employees (Stanko and Werner 16). These "hidden costs" can add up to six or seven million dollars a year for a typical large company, according to a recent survey of Fortune 500 companies (Stanko and Werner 16). 5

Because of such potential losses, many companies have chosen to take special measures to avoid problems with sexual harassment before they occur. Such measures include sexual-harassment policies and procedures, as well as training sessions to educate employees and to reinforce these company policies. Victims are also encouraged to come forward as early as possible so that employers have a chance to remedy the situation before it gets out of hand (Martell and Sullivan 8). Prior to 1991, sexual-harassment victims were often asked by their employers simply to remain silent (Martell and Sullivan 8). 6

The media have been another great source of education con-   7
cerning sexual harassment. Since 1991, the year Justice Clarence
Thomas, then a Supreme Court nominee, was accused of having sexually harassed his former colleague Anita Hill, the media have paid especially close attention to the subject. Later that same year, the "U. S.
Navy's Tailhook scandal, involving the sexual harassment of women at-
tending a convention of naval aviators" (Nelton 24) also became prominent in the news. The highly publicized nature of these two incidents
made sexual harassment a much discussed public issue that sparked debate and encouraged victims to come forth.

One journalist has argued that the rise in reported sexual-   8
harassment complaints is actually a sort of illusion caused by insufficient
research, since "research on this topic has only been undertaken since
the 1970s" (Burke 23). Although this statement is largely true, it is only
true because the Civil Rights Act did not exist until 1964. How could
sexual harassment be measured and researched if it was not even acknowledged yet by society?

It has also been suggested that the trend is the result of a greater   9
percentage of women in the workplace (Martell and Sullivan 5). This
may be a sufficient argument since women report sexual harassment in
a significantly greater number of cases than men do (men report roughly
one-tenth of what women report). It has been noted, however, that
there has been a rise in sexual-harassment complaints reported by male
victims as well recently. According to the Equal Employment Opportunity Commission, the number of sexual-harassment complaints filed
annually by men has more than doubled from 1989 to 1993 (Corey).
Sexual harassment is by no means a new occurrence. It has most likely
existed since workplace environments have existed. Yes, that there are
more women in the workplace today has likely increased the percentage of women workers being sexually harassed, but it is also very plausible that the rise in reported incidents of sexual harassment is due to
increased awareness of sexual harassment and the steps that one can
legally take to stop it.

It has taken thirty years, but American society seems to be mak-   10
ing significant progress in bringing a halt to a serious problem. *Sexual
harassment*, a phrase that was unfamiliar to most of us only a few years
ago, is now mentioned almost daily on television, in newspapers, as well
as in pamphlets handed out in high school homerooms. We can only
hope that the problem will end if we continue to hear about, to read
about, and, most importantly to talk about sexual harassment and its
negative consequences as we educate each other about sexual harass-

ment. Then, perhaps someday, sexual harassment can be stopped altogether.

Works Cited

Burke, Ronald J. "Incidence and Consequences of Sexual Harassment in a Professional Services Firm." *Employee Counselling Today* Feb. 1995: 23–29.

Corey, Mary. "On-the-Job Sexism Isn't Just a Man's Sin Anymore." *Houston Chronicle* 30 Aug. 1993: D1.

Nelton, Sharon. "Sexual Harassment: Reducing the Risks." *Nation's Business* Mar. 1995: 24–26.

Martell, Kathryn, and George Sullivan. "Strategies for Managers to Recognize and Remedy Sexual Harassment." *Industrial Management* May/June 1994: 5–8.

Stanko, Brian B., and Charles A. Werner. "Sexual Harassment: What Is It? How to Prevent It." *National Public Accountant* June 1995: 14–16.

"Workplace Bias Lawsuits." *USA Today* 30 Nov. 1994: B2.

CHAPTER 10

INTERPRETING STORIES

*O*nce you learn how to play the "literary game," interpreting stories actually can be fun. Both of the essays in this chapter show writers genuinely engaged with the stories they're writing about, and that engagement translates as fun.

Both Sarah Hawkins and Margaret Tate present strong interpretations. Speculate how these writers arrived at these interpretations by imagining Sarah Hawkins, for instance, responding to D. H. Lawrence's "In Love," noticing initially that each character's version of love is not quite the same. We might picture her returning to the story to examine it more closely, committing gradually to her response as she discovers convincing textual evidence that supports and extends it. In the process, she begins to notice a larger thematic pattern in Lawrence's characters which eventually becomes the focus of her essay, an extremely plausible interpretation that evolved from an initial "gut" response.

The structure of Hawkins's essay reveals something of her reading strategy. She responds to words, motifs, and statements that intrigue her, interpreting them for the way they suggest and contribute to the pattern of "being in love" that forms her thesis. Her structural plan is straightforward: Examine each character in turn for the mode of "being in love" that he or she exemplifies.

Margaret Tate's essay on Susan Glaspell's "A Jury of Her Peers" is interesting on a number of counts. She begins with a forecasting statement at the end of the first paragraph but doesn't articulate her thesis—that "men and women vary greatly in their perception of things"—until the last paragraph. It's as if the forecasting statement sets her off and running to gather the evidence that finally "adds up" to her conclusion.

To read fun into Tate's essay, we might imagine that, on her first encounter, she noticed a discrepancy in the way male and female characters in the story act and react to events. She might have followed up this initial response by *rereading the text and discovering a larger pattern of irony that eventually developed into her thesis and supporting analysis. It isn't just Tate's skillful literary perception and creative interpretation that make the essay succeed. It's the way she puts everything together. Instead of simply collecting examples that interest her in the text and loosely arranging them, Tate interconnects her ideas with strong supporting evidence in a tight, coherent tapestry of meaning that enriches and extends her initial insight.*

"In Love": The Story

"In Love," a short story by D. H. Lawrence, opens with twenty-five-year-old Hester anxiously fretting about a weekend visit to the farm cottage of her fiancé, Joe. On this day a month before the wedding, Hester's younger sister, Henrietta, confronts her and tells her point-blank that she needs to snap out of her pout and "either put a better face on it, or . . . don't go." Although Hester does make the trip, she is never comfortable with her decision.

The crux of Hester's problem is that she and Joe had been good friends for years before she finally promised to marry him. Hester had always respected Joe as a hardworking, "decent" fellow, but, now that they are to marry, she finds him changed. What she detests is the fact that, in her view, he seems to have made "the wretched mistake of falling 'in love' with her." To Hester, this notion of being in love, accentuated by all of Joe's "lovey-dovey" attempts to cuddle and snuggle and kiss, is completely idiotic and ridiculous.

After she arrives at Joe's farm cottage, Hester avoids his advances by asking him to play the piano. As he concentrates on his fingering, she slips outside into the night air and, when Joe comes looking for her, remains hidden in a tree. Alone in the dark, Hester falls into a fit of internal questioning, doubt, and upset concerning "the mess" her life seems to have become. Then suddenly, in the midst of her anxiety, who should arrive but Henrietta, claiming she is in the neighborhood on a visit to a friend down the road. Hester leaps at the chance to join Henrietta and thus escape her entrapment with Joe. When Joe hears this, however, he responds angrily, accusing the two sisters of playing a "game."

In the confrontation that follows, Hester and Joe honestly speak the truth of their feelings to each other for the first time. Hester tells Joe she detests his "making love" to her. Joe responds that she's mistaken, that he was in fact not "in love" with her but was behaving in such a manner only because he thought that "it was expected." In the conversation, Joe goes on to reveal his dilemma and his true feelings about Hester: "What are you to do," he says, "When you know a girl's rather strict, and you like her for it?"

In speaking the truth of their hearts to each other for the first time, the couple is able to reveal the depth of their feelings. They recognize that they've betrayed the intimacy of their relationship because they've acted on the basis of expectations rather than on the basis of genuine emotion. By acknowledging these facts, the couple is able to reach new understanding. Seeing Joe's honest love, Hester feels herself responding to him and, in the end, decides to stay with him. She will accept whatever he does, she says, as long as he really loves her.

IN LOVE

Sarah Hawkins

■

University of California, San Diego
La Jolla, California

F or most people, the phrase *in love* brings many rosy pictures   1
to mind: a young man looking into the eyes of the girl he loves, a couple walking along the beach holding hands, two people making sacrifices to be together. These stereotypes about what love is and how
lovers "should" act can be very harmful. In his short story "In Love,"
D. H. Lawrence uses the three main characters to embody his theme
that love is experienced in a unique way by every couple and that there
isn't a "normal" or "proper" way to be in love.

Hester, her fiancé, Joe, and her sister, Henrietta, all approach and   2
respond to love in different ways. Hester is unwilling to compromise
what she really feels for Joe, but she is pressured by her own notions of
how a young woman in her situation should feel. Joe appears to be the
typical young man in love. He seems at ease with the situation, and his
moves are so predictable they could have come straight from a movie
script. But when he is confronted and badgered by Hester and Henrietta, he admits that he was only putting on an act and feels regret for
not being honest with Hester. Henrietta is the mouthpiece for all of society's conceptions of love. She repeatedly asks Hester to be "normal"
and secretly worries that Hester will call off the wedding. Henrietta is
like a mother hen, always making sure that Hester is doing the right
thing (in Henrietta's opinion, anyway).

Hester and Joe are, in a sense, playing a game with each other.   3

Both are acting on what they feel is expected of them now that they are engaged, as if how they really feel about each other is unimportant. It is only when Hester and Joe finally talk honestly about their relationship that they realize they have been in love all along in their own unique way.

Hester, ever the practical one, becomes more and more frustrated 4
with "Joe's love-making" (650). She feels ridiculous, as if she is just a toy, but at the same time she feels she should respond to Joe, ". . . because she believed that a nice girl would have been only too delighted to go and sit 'there' " (650). Rather than doing what she wants, enjoying a nice, comfortable relationship with Joe, Hester does what she feels she ought to. She says that she ought to like Joe's lovemaking even though she doesn't really know why. "Ought" is a key issue for Hester because it involves so many conflicting feelings. Despite her practical and independent nature, Hester is still troubled by what society would think.

Lawrence seems to be suggesting a universal theme here. If Hes- 5
ter, with such firm ideas about what she wants, is so troubled by what society dictates, then how much more are we, as generally less objective and more tractable people, affected by society's standards? Hester's is a dilemma everyone faces.

At the heart of Hester's confusion is Joe, whose personality was 6
so different before they became engaged that Hester might not have gotten engaged if she had known how Joe would change: "Six months ago, Hester would have enjoyed it [being alone with Joe]. They were so perfectly comfortable together, he and she" (649). But by cuddling and petting, Joe has ruined the comfortable relationship that he and Hester had enjoyed. The most surprising line in the story is Hester's assertion that "[t]he very fact of his being in love with me proves that he doesn't love me" (652). Here, Hester makes a distinction between really loving someone and just putting on an act of being *in* love, a distinction that she sees in Joe's new "Rudolf Valentino" mode of being "in love." Hester feels hurt that Joe would treat her as a typical girl rather than as the young woman she really is.

Hester is a reluctant player in the "love game" until the end of 7
the story when she confronts Joe and blurts out, "I absolutely can't stand your making love to me, if that is what you call the business" (656–57). Her use of the word *business* is significant because it refers to a chore, something that has to be done. Hester regards Joe's lovemaking as if it were merely a job to be completed. When Joe apologizes, Hester sees his patient, real love for her, and she begins to have the same feelings

for him again. When she says, "I don't mind what you do if you love me really," (660) Hester, by compromising, shows the nature of their love for each other.

Lawrence uses Joe to show a typical response to society's pressures. Joe obediently plays the role of the husband-to-be. He exhibits all the preconceived images one may have about a man about to be married. In trying to fit the expectations of others, Joe sacrifices his straightforwardness and the honesty that Hester valued so much in him. Although Joe's actions don't seem to be so bad in and of themselves, in the context of his relationship with Hester they are completely out of place. His piano playing, for example, inspires Hester to remark that Joe's love games would be impossible to handle after the music he played. The music represents something that is pure and true—in contrast to the new, hypocritical Joe. Joe doesn't seem to be aware of Hester's feelings until she comes forward with them at the end of the story. The humiliation he suffers makes him silent, and he is described several times as "wooden," implying stubbornness and solidity. It is out of this "woodenness" that a changed Joe appears. At first the word suggests his defensiveness for his bruised ego, but then as Joe begins to see Hester's point about being truly in love, his "woodenness" is linked to his solidity and stability, qualities that represent for Hester the old Joe. Once Joe gets his mind off the love game, the "simple intimacy" of their relationship is revealed to him, and he desires Hester, not in a fleeting way, but in a way that one desires something that was almost lost. 8

Henrietta serves as the antagonist in this story because it is through her that society's opinions come clear. In almost the first line of text, Henrietta, looking at Hester, states, "If I had such a worried look on my face, when I was going down to spend the weekend with the man I was engaged to—and going to be married to in a month—well! I should either try and change my face or hide my feelings, or something" (647). With little regard for Hester's feelings, Henrietta is more concerned that Hester have the right attitude. Although Henrietta herself is not married, the fact that Hester, who is twenty-five, is soon to be married is a relief to her. Not wanting her sister to be an "old maid," Henrietta does all she can to make sure the weekend runs smoothly. She acts as though Hester were her responsibility and even offers to come with Hester to take the "edge off the intimacy" (648). Being young, Henrietta hasn't really formed her own views of life or love yet. As a result, she easily believes the traditional statements society makes about love. When Hester says that she can't stand Joe's being in love with her, Henrietta keeps responding that a man is supposed to be in love with 9 the woman he marries. She doesn't understand the real love that Joe and Hester eventually feel but only the "ought-tos" of love imposed by society. It is unclear at the end of the story whether Henrietta really recognizes the new bond between Hester and Joe or whether she leaves, glad that they are happy together, but not really knowing why.

What society and common beliefs dictate about being in love   10
isn't really important. In order to be happy, couples must find their own unique bond of love and not rely on others' opinions or definitions. Joe and Hester come to this realization only after they are hurt and left unfulfilled as a result of the "love game" they play with each other. Hester knew how she really felt from the beginning, but pressure about what she *ought* to feel worried her. Joe willingly went along with the game until he realized how important their simple intimacy really was. In the end, Hester and Joe are "in love" not because of the love games that Joe started with their engagement but because of an intimate friendship that had been growing all along.

Works Cited

Lawrence, D. H. "In Love." *The Complete Short Stories.* Vol. 3. New York: Penguin, 1977.

"A Jury of Her Peers": The Story

Susan Glaspell's short story, "A Jury of Her Peers," begins when three men and two women—Mr. Peters, the county sheriff; Mr. Henderson, the county attorney; and Mr. Hale, a farmer; along with two wives, Mrs. Peters and Mrs. Hale—begin to investigate the death of a farm neighbor, John Wright, whom they believe was murdered the previous day by his wife, Mrs. Wright. Although there is no direct evidence linking her to the crime, she is nevertheless jailed on suspicion of murder.

At the Wright farmhouse, the county attorney asks Mr. Hale, the man who by chance discovered the murder, to recount his experience at the farmhouse. Mr. Hale describes how he found Mrs. Wright sitting in a rocking chair as she calmly told him that Mr. Wright was upstairs dead from a rope around his neck.

As the three men search the farmhouse for evidence that might establish a motive for the crime, Mrs. Peters and Mrs. Hale sit in Mrs. Wright's kitchen. With attentive eyes, they keenly observe domestic details that begin to reveal a pattern of meaning that the men overlook. As they continue to look around, the details begin to speak volumes about the emotional lives and marital relationship of Mr. and Mrs. Wright. Mrs. Peters and Mrs. Hale notice the uncharacteristic dirty pans and towels in the kitchen, neither of which fit Mrs. Wright's character as a careful housekeeper. They note a half-full bag of sugar that, again, is uncharacteristic, suggesting an interrupted task. They find a single square on Mrs. Wright's quilt that is raggedly sewn—just one, amidst a field of perfectly sewn pieces—that suggests the seamstress had to be out of sorts with herself.

As these domestic details add up, they gain significance for the women while the men scoff and dismiss their concerns as simplistic and typical of "women." Finally, when the women discover a birdcage with its door broken and then at the bottom of the sewing basket a dead canary wrapped in silk, its neck wrung, they realize they have stumbled upon the motive for the murder. Bound up in the details of violence and dishonor—the husband killed the wife's canary—Mrs. Peters and Mrs. Hale discover the joyless horror Mrs. Wright endured in her marriage to her "hard," uncaring husband. They realize John Wright was the man who killed not a canary, but also the spirit of his wife, a woman who had been a beautiful singer—a songbird—in her youth. Mrs. Peters and Mrs. Hale draw on personal experiences to empathize with Mrs. Wright. Mrs. Peters recalls the raging desire to "hurt" the boy who killed her kitten when she was a girl, and Mrs. Hale recalls the "stillness" she felt when her first baby died, likening it to the stillness that Mrs. Wright must have endured in her loveless marriage.

In the end, Mrs. Peters's and Mrs. Hale's empathy for Mrs. Wright is so deep that when the men return to collect them to leave, the women look at each other and Mrs. Hale quickly stuffs the bird's body in her coat pocket. Without concrete evidence to establish a motive for murder, they know a jury will not convict the woman. Although the men believe their wives are "married to the law," Mrs. Peters and Mrs. Hale act as Mrs. Wright's first jury—a true jury of her peers, relying on experience, intuition, and empathy rather than legal reasoning to find justice in their world.

IRONY AND INTUITION IN "A JURY OF HER PEERS"

Margaret Tate

■

DeKalb College
Decatur, Georgia

T hough men and women are now recognized as generally   1
equal in talent and intelligence, when Susan Glaspell wrote "A Jury of
Her Peers" in 1917, it was not so. In this turn-of-the-century, rural mid-
western setting, women were often barely educated and possessed virtually no political or economic power. And, being the "weaker sex,"
there was not much they could do about it. Relegated to home and
hearth, women found themselves at the mercy of the more powerful
men in their lives. Ironically, it is just this type of powerless existence,
perhaps, that over the ages developed in women a power with which
they could baffle and frustrate their male counterparts: a sixth sense—
an inborn trait commonly known as "women's intuition." In Glaspell's
story, ironic situations contrast male and female intuition, illustrating
that Minnie Wright is more fairly judged by "a jury of her peers."

"A Jury of Her Peers" first uses irony to illustrate the contrast be-   2
tween male and female intuition when the men go to the farmhouse
looking for clues to the murder of John Wright, but it is the women
who find them. In the Wright household, the men are searching for
something out of the ordinary, an obvious indication that Minnie has
been enraged or provoked into killing her husband. Their intuition does
not tell them that their wives, because they are women, can help them
gain insight into what has occurred between John and his wife. They

bring Mrs. Hale and Mrs. Peters along merely to tend to the practical matters, considering them needlessly preoccupied with trivial things and even too unintelligent to make a contribution to the investigation, as Mr. Hale's derisive question reveals: "Would the women know a clue if they did come upon it?" (289).

Ironically, they do discover the clue to the murder of John   3
Wright. For while the men are looking actively for the "smoking gun," the women are confronted with more subtle clues in spite of themselves and even try to hide from each other what they intuitively know. But they do not fool each other for long, as Glaspell describes: "Their eyes met—something flashed to life, passed between them; then, as if with an effort, they seemed to pull away from each other" (295). However, they cannot pull away, for they are bound by a power they do not even comprehend: "We all go through the same things—it's all just a different kind of the same thing! . . . why do you and I *understand*? Why do we *know*—what we know this minute?" (303). They do not realize that it is intuition they share, that causes them to "[see] into things, [to see] through a thing to something else. . . ." (294). Though sympathetic to Minnie Wright, the women cannot deny the damning clues that lead them to the inescapable conclusion of her guilt.

If it is ironic that the women find the clues, it is even more ironic   4
that they find them in the mundane household items to which the men attribute so little significance. "Nothing here but kitchen things," the men mistakenly think (287). Because of their weak intuition, they do not see the household as indicative of John's and Minnie's characters. They do not see beyond the cheerless home to John Wright's grim nature, nor do the dilapidated furnishings provide them with a clue to his penurious habits. Minnie's depression and agitation are not apparent to them in the dismal, half-cleaned kitchen; instead, they consider Minnie an inept, lazy housekeeper. Oddly, for all their "snoopin' round and criticizin' " (290), the three gentlemen do not have a clue.

The women, on the other hand, "used to worrying over trifles"   5
(287), do attach importance to the "everyday things" (299), and, looking around the cheerless kitchen, they see many examples of the miserably hard existence of Minnie Wright. Knowing the pride a woman takes in her home, they see Minnie's kitchen not as dirty, but as half-cleaned, and the significance of this is not lost on them. And, upon discovering the erratic quilt stitching, they are alarmed. Also, they cannot dismiss the broken birdcage as just a broken birdcage. They instinctively know, as the men do not, that Minnie desperately needs a lively crea-

ture to brighten up such a loveless home. Upon finding these clues, ironically hidden in everyday objects, the women piece them together with a thread of intuition and create a blanket of guilt that covers the hapless Minnie Wright.

Though there is irony in the fact that the women, not the men, find the clues, and there is irony in the fact that they are found in everyday household things, most ironic is the fact that John Wright meets the same fate he has inflicted on the poor bird, illustrating that he is perhaps the least intuitive of all the men in the story. John Wright never sees beyond his own needs to the needs of his wife. He does not understand her need for a pretty creature to fill the void created by her lonely, childless existence. Not content to kill just Minnie's personality (". . . she was [once] kind of like a bird herself. Real sweet and pretty" [299]), he kills her canary, leaving her with the deafening silence of the lonesome prairie. Minnie has endured many years of misery at the hands of John Wright, but he pushes her too far when he kills the bird. Then, ironically, he gets the "peace and quiet" (283) he values over her happiness.

John Wright lacks the intuition to understand his wife's love of her bird, but the two women do not. They understand that she needed the bird to fill the still air with song and lessen her loneliness. After discovering the dead bird, they do not blame her for killing John. The dead bird reminds Mrs. Peters of a traumatic episode from her childhood:

> "When I was a girl," said Mrs. Peters, under her breath, "my kitten— there was a boy took a hatchet, and before my eyes—before I could get there. . . . If they hadn't held me back, I would have . . . hurt him." (301–02)

The women see the reason for Minnie's murderous impulse, but they know that the men lack the insight to ever fully understand her situation or her motivation; therefore, in hiding the bird, by their silence, they acquit Minnie Wright.

Through the ironic situations in "A Jury of Her Peers," Glaspell clearly illustrates a world in which men and women vary greatly in their perception of things. She shows men as often superficial in the way they perceive the world, lacking the depth of intuition that women use as a means of self-preservation to see themselves and the world more clearly. Without the heightened perspective on life that this knowledge of human nature gives them, women might not stand a chance. Against the power and domination of men, they often find themselves as defenseless and vulnerable as Minnie's poor bird.

Works Cited

Glaspell, Susan. "A Jury of Her Peers." *Lifted Masks and Other Works.* Ed. Eric S. Rabkin. Ann Arbor: U of Michigan P, 1993.

A NOTE ON THE COPYEDITING

We all know that the work of professional writers rarely appears in print without first being edited. But what about student writing—especially essays that are presented *as models* of student writing? Do these get edited too?

This is not as clear-cut an issue as it may first appear. While it's easy to draw an analogy with professional writing and simply declare that "all published writing gets edited," there are some important differences between student and professional writing. For one thing, the student writing is presented *as student writing*. That is, it's offered to the reader as an example of the kind of writing students can and do produce in a writing class. And since most students don't have the benefit of a professional editor to read their work before it's graded, their work may not be as polished as the models they see in textbooks.

For another, students whose work appears in publications like these rarely have the opportunity to participate in the editorial process. Publication schedules being what they are, text authors and editors often don't know exactly what they want in terms of example essays until late in the process, and by then they may be so immersed in their own revising that it's difficult, if not impossible, to supervise twenty-five or more student writers as well.

For these reasons, student writers are usually simply asked to sign a statement, transferring to the publisher "all rights to my essay, subject to final editing by the publisher," and don't see their work again until it appears in print. That makes the situation somewhat problematic.

But publishing student essays without editing is equally problematic. Every composition teacher knows that even the best papers, the A+ essays, aren't perfect. But readers of published prose, accustomed to the conventions

174

of edited American English, aren't always so generous. The shift in tense that may be seen as a simple lapse in a student narrative becomes a major distraction in a published piece. Rather than preserve that tense shift in the interest of "absolute fidelity" to the student's work, it is more in keeping with the spirit and purpose of the enterprise to edit the passage. After all, the rest of the evidence indicates that the student is a strong writer, and would likely accede to the change if it were called to his or her attention.

In this respect, editing student essays should be seen not as a violation of the student's work but as a courtesy to the writer. True, some essays require more editing than others—perhaps because the student did not have as much opportunity to revise—but none in this collection have been altered significantly. In fact, every attempt has been made to respect the student's choices.

To give you an inside look at the editing process, we reproduce here the originally submitted version of Erick Young's essay, "Only She" (p. 170), along with the St. Martin's editor's "blue pencil" markings. It might be interesting to compare this early version with the final edited version printed on pages 41–45. What changes were made, and why? Were all of them necessary? If you were the writer, how would you react to these changes?

Finally, if you are a writer whose work has undergone editorial revision—perhaps as a result of peer critique—you might think about how the process felt to you. Did you appreciate your editor's work? Resent it? What did you learn from it? If you're like most of us, you probably realized that it's natural to resist criticism, but necessary to accept it. In other words, you learned to think of yourself as a writer.

SAMPLE COPYEDITING

> Erick Young
>
> Person Essay
>
> Rewrite

Only She

Those eyes. No no, deep, dark brown. Hardly a
wrinkle around them. Soft, smooth ~~looking~~ skin. And those
eyebrows. Neither thick nor thin; just bold two curved
punctuat~~ion marks gracing~~ her facial expressions with a
certain ~~extra accent~~ something. Surprise, amusement up would shoot
one of the brows, the right one I believe, just slightly,
accompanied by a mischievous little smirk ~~that would curl
onto her lips~~. Anger, irritation up and inward shot both
brows, tightly pressed, followed by a sharp "What d'ya
want? Don't bother me!" She never really meant it
though; ~~she~~ it was just saying her way of "hello." Even though she wore
glasses she could still see all, with or without them.
Her deep, dark brown eyes were no ordinary ~~little masses
of flesh and tissue~~ eyes; no, within those deep wells rested a
pair of magic orbs, two miniature crystal balls that

176

could peer into your mind, and read all your little
thoughts. Some thought she had psychic powers. She knew
what you were thinking, or at least ~~so many times,~~ she
always seemed to know   even   most
~~knew~~ what I was thinking, ~~all of~~ my complex, inexplicable
thoughts. And that was all that seemed to matter at the
time. Only she, only Sonia Koujakian, ~~only~~ Mrs. K.

I do not recall the first time I noticed her at
                                              a
school, but Mrs. K was not one to blend into ~~the~~ crowd,
                            the
~~for very long.~~ Briskly walking across ~~our~~ school's
rotunda, I would see her, tall and lean, wearing a skirt
and a mauve-colored raincoat, holding a stuffed beige
handbag in one hand, and a bright red coffee pot in the
other. She seemed so confident, always looking straight
ahead ~~rather than down~~ as she walked about ~~the~~ school.
Perhaps it was her hair that first caught my eye. It was
              a mix of
short, ~~almost spiked, with its~~ light brown and gray, ~~hairs~~
                         1 almost spiked.
combed slightly up. Not the typical sort of hairstyle for
an English teacher at our school. It set her apart ~~though~~
and made her look, dynamic. Already I knew that she was
somebody special.
              PSAT
The ~~beckon to take the Preliminary Scholastic~~
                her into my life
~~Aptitude Test~~ brought ~~us together briefly~~ for the first
time, in my sophomore year, ~~allowing me to get a small~~
~~taste of Mrs. K's personality.~~ Even though she was the
                                              ed
senior English teacher, she ~~made an open~~ offer to coach

177

any undaunted sophomores or juniors after school for the nefarious "SAT jr." Trying to be the savvy student, I joined ~~two other friends and accepted her offer. Only~~ a small group ~~of us~~ gathered in her cove after/school ~~the following afternoons and~~ practiced vocabulary drills and sentence completions. Mrs. K would scold us on the finer points of grammar (when we reviewed our errors) ~~throwing at~~ us her "Come on, get with the production!" ~~expression.~~ Not the typical reaction from a ~~person one hardly knew;~~ ~~all the little formalities I had come to expect in a~~ ~~teacher student relationships had been thrown out the~~ ~~window with Mrs. K.~~ She treated us like peers, and would say to us what was on her mind without ~~any~~ pretense, ~~niceties,~~ or euphenisms. We could do the same, if we had the ~~stomach~~ to try. Her casual disposition made me feel both relaxed and nervous; ~~I did not know~~ how to act around her, whether to joke and tease her, or respect and honor her. ~~Most of my friends felt the same way.~~ We all ~~felt~~ however, she ~~simply~~ was ~~down-to-Earth,~~ as down-to-Earth as they come, ~~friends, teachers, or anyone. Soon,~~ ~~the prep sessions were over and it would not be until~~ two years later as an older and wiser senior, ~~that~~ I would get ~~the~~ full ~~taste~~ of Mrs. K's personality.

My first day in Mrs. K's class left much to be desired. Most of my classmates just ~~sat around waiting,~~

Inserted editor's marks: who · # · to · as · giving · look · ever · teacher; · pleasantry, · m · guts · none of us knew · agreed, that · a · dose · I entered to find

178

and laughing, joking. The first-day-of-school jitters had become passé, and the smugness that comes with seniordom dominated the room. It was a convention of Alfred E. Neumans, and the nonchalant air of "What Me Worry?" filled the classroom. Some students, however, sat very quietly. These were wise ones; they'd heard about Mrs. K before. Academic tensions hovered like the inevitable black storm cloud above Room 5C3. There was a small fear of the unknown and the unexpected nudging about in my stomach as I sat at the far end of the center table. Strange how this was the only classroom in the entire building to have six huge wooden tables instead of forty individual little desks; someone must have wanted it that way. For once I was not too anxious to sit up front. Suddenly the chattering diminished. Mrs. K was coming.

In she ambled, with her stuffed handbag and bright red coffee pot, wearing a skirt and the mauve raincoat; she was just as I had remembered. She scanned the room, and up went her right eyebrow. A most peculiar "I-know-what-you-are-up-to" smirk was our first greeting. Now I was nervous.

"All right ladies and gentlemen, I want to see if

you belong in my class," she began~~, in a soft but earnest voice.~~ "Take out a pen and lots of paper." Pause. "Now don't get too worried over this, since you are all geniuses anyway. You know, if you've got it you've got it, if you don't. . ." ~~Her shoulders~~ *She* shrugged. Pause. "Some of you know you don't really belong in here," she chided~~, as she~~ point~~ed~~*ing* her finger, "and it's time you stopped getting put in Honors English just because ~~you have a little star by your name in the role book, meaning~~ you passed some little test ~~back~~ *silly* in second grade. Well now we're going to see what you can do." ~~she said matter-of-factly, arms akimbo, right brow up.~~ "Okay now, stop and think for a moment, and get those ~~wonderful~~ creative juices going. I want you to write me a paper telling me the origin of the English language. You can be as creative as you want. Make up something if you have to $\frac{1}{m}$ two cavemen grunting ~~to~~ *at* each other, I don't care. You have until the end of the period. Go."

It was not the most encouraging welcome. For a moment the whole class just sort of slumped in their seats suddenly ~~phazed and drained~~ *drained* of all vitality and hopes of a relaxed senior year. Blank faces abounded. ~~Mine was one of them.~~ *included* I had no idea what to write. The origin of the English language? Being "creative" seemed too risky. What ever happened to the good ol' five-

180

paragraph essay with specific examples? Well I didn't have any specific examples anyway. I remember staring at a sheet of white paper, then scrawling down some incoherent mumbo-jumbo. I wanted to impress her, too much. ~~I choked, and was doomed to a dismal dungeon of drudgery. I blew it with Mrs. K.~~ "It was nice knowing you," I sig**h**ned as I handed in my paper. What a first day.

That first day ~~of class~~ **with Mrs. K** would not be my last₀ ~~with Mrs. K~~ (fortunately,) A ~~poor performance on the first pressure writing was not a notice of termination but rather an early warning of possible eviction.~~ **Although** The class size shrunk **over** the following days as some students ran for their academic lives, I was not prepared to leave. I knew Mrs. K's class would be an arduous English journey, but I could never let myself miss it. It would be a journey well worth taking.

As the weeks continued, tidbits of Mrs. K's colorful past and philosophy about life would somehow always creep into ~~our~~ lectures and class discussions. We found out she had served as a volunteer nurse in a Japan~~-based combat hospital~~ **combat hospital in** and had "seen it all, **m**even grown men cry." During the **19**'60s a wider Mrs. K could be seen cruising the streets of San Francisco ~~atop~~ **on** motorcycle, decked out in long spiked boots and short spiked hair. She later traded in her motorcycle and boots for a Fiat and white Reeboks⊙ ~~though⁋~~ And there was a running joke about her age. Mrs. K could not be much ~~younger~~ **less** than ~~her mid-forties,~~ **forty-five** but just as Jack Benny was forever ~~39~~ **thirty-nine**, she was forever ~~28~~ **twenty-eight**. One of her T-shirts said so. Twenty-eight was a good year, ~~for her~~ **she** she would tell us, but never quite why. **explained**

I would come to deeply trust and respect this ~~seemingly~~ eccentric lady⊙ ~~while the school year progressed.~~ I guess I have <u>Oedipus Rex</u> to thank for our first ~~close~~ **out-of-class** meeting. We had to compose an extensive essay on the Oedipus ~~T~~rilogy, (much of) **on** which our semester grade would be based. Foolishly I chose to write on the most ~~difficult~~ abstract topic, ~~concerning~~ predestination and divine justice. I toiled for days, ~~inflicting upon~~ **torturing** myself ~~a sort deranged mental torture~~ **up with some** trying to come ~~to~~ definitive conclusions~~es~~. **Finally** I realized my struggle was merely carrying my mind farther and farther adrift in a sea of confusion. I needed someone to rescue me; I needed Mrs. K.

We arranged to meet in the Faculty Commons, a small, smoky room of teachers with ~~their~~ red pens at work and administrators shooting the breeze over lunch. I crept inside with notes in hand and took a seat⊙ ~~amongst the haze.~~ She soon arrived, holding a tuna-on-wheat, a chocolate chip cookie, and **the** a red coffee pot. "I hope you don't mind if I eat while we ~~discuss~~ talk," she ~~mentioned off handly,~~ said "but if you do, I'm going to eat anyway." Smile.

We talked the whole lunch period. I felt awkward at first, actually struggling to explain why ~~I was~~ I'd been struggling ~~before~~ with the assignment. But then Mrs. K the Mentor emerged -- soft spoken, introspective, wise. I opened up to her. We sat beside ~~one~~ each another at that table, reflecting on predestination, divine justice, and life. A ray of sunshine cut through ~~my~~ s cloud of confusion. Our reflections ~~were~~ interrupted by the lunch bell, but we ~~later~~ continued after school. Two days and two drafts later, I had gained more than just a deep understanding of Oedipus Rex: I gained a friend. What was it about this woman that enabled me to reveal a different part of myself? Never before had I ~~ever~~ spoken so openly about my thoughts, ~~and~~ or about myself. Most people did not understand ~~what~~ my cares and thoughts. ~~I was contemplating.~~ But she understood. ~~Oftentimes I did not have to explain much, her crystal balls would perform their magic.~~

I would go back to room 5C3 many afternoons later to sort my thoughts. To her I was no longer Erick but Hamlet, ~~deemed~~ because of my pensive and complex nature. "Okay Hamlet, what's on your mind?" our conversations would begin. ~~It seemed~~ every writing assignment became an excuse to spend time after school talking and reflecting,

~~with just~~ me at the wood table, ~~and~~ ~~she~~ wh*en* at h*er* stool. We

digressed on everything from <u>Paradise Lost</u> to Shakespeare

to ~~Robert Frost's~~ "The Road Not Taken," ~~these many~~

~~afternoons.~~ Sometimes other students would come

~~afterschool~~ for help on their papers, ~~but~~ *and* I would always

let them go first, so that I could be the last left.

~~Sometimes~~ *Often* I would ~~receive small lessons in life~~ learn about more

~~afterschool.~~ "Life's not black and white, it's a hazy

gray, and you've always got to use that wonderful piece

of machinery God gave you and question things because

nothing is clear cut," ~~and learn more about this world~~

than just literature: I noticed my perceptions changing,

as well as my writing style. More of my character entered

my writing, and the Mr. Detached Impartiality persona I

once favored faded into the background. Being "creative"

no longer seemed risky. She told me to put more *to*

myself in my creations, and I listened.

~~Towards~~ *near* the ~~close~~ *end* of my senior year, I asked her

about her favorite novel, ~~during~~ one ~~last~~ afternoon. "Oh,

without a doubt, <u>Les Misérables</u>," she replied. "But I

never could find an unedited version." ~~Three days later~~

~~at the end of~~ *On* Graduation Day, ~~while~~ *in* a sea of ~~teary eyed~~

seniors hugg*ing* one another, and red and blue ~~motorboaards~~ mortarboards

~~sailed~~ *sailing* through the air, I searched through the crowd for

Mrs. K, and handed her a small box. ~~Wrapped~~ inside with a

~~card, and a~~ long thank-you on the cover ~~,~~ was a new copy *of*
<u>Les Miserables</u>, unedited and unabridged.

  I doubt I will come across many others like Mrs. K. **that** ~~in my life,~~ Only she would sit with me one-on-one, and review every minute detail of a draft. Only she would give up ~~many~~ an afternoon to just ~~sit down~~ shoot the breeze. Only she could I call a mentor, a confidant, and a friend. I still think of Mrs. K. Sometimes, when the pressures of college come crashing down, and the order of life seems to have run amok, I go to my room and slowly close the door and my eyes, sit down, and talk with Mrs. K.

  "Okay Hamlet, what's on your mind. . ."

Acknowledgments

We gratefully acknowledge the following instructors, who kindly submitted some of their students' best work for this collection.

Vance Aandahl, Metropolitan State College of Denver
Cheryl Alton, St. Xavier University
Karen Aubrey, Augusta College
Nancy Benjamin, Augusta College
Lee Bollinger, Augusta College
Richard Boyd, University of California at Riverside
Christine Brandel, Bowling Green State University
Karla Brown, Hawkeye Community College
Richard Bullock, Wright State University
Grace Bailey Burneko, Augusta College
Mary Ellen Byrne, Ocean County College
Sandy Cavanaugh, Hopkinsville Community College
Peggy Cheney, Augusta College
Daniel Clark, Northern Kentucky University
John M. Clark, Bowling Green State University
Joan Costello, Inver Hills Community College
Christopher Cotton, Bowling Green State University
Rick Davis, Augusta College
Jane L. Dockery, Wright State University
Gail Dadik, Arizona State University
Janet Kay Dillon, Kansas State University
Erin Echols, Augusta College
Suzanne Emery, Bowling Green State University

Nancy Ethridge, Boise State University
Beth Fanning, Augusta College
M. E. Gandy, Bishop State Community College
Judith Gardner, University of Texas at San Antonio
Peter Goggin, Arizona State University
Dorie Goldman, Arizona State University
Gloria Greenbaum, Augusta College
Ron Greene, Guilford Technical Community College
Barbara Grogan-Barone, George Mason University
Professor Hankinson, Mount San Jacinto College
Mitzi Harris, Western Wyoming Community College
Arthur Henne, Pennsylvania State University–York Campus
Jack Hettinger, College of Mount St. Joseph
Michael Hricik, Westmoreland County Community College
Kathleen Jernquist, Brown University
Barbara Josephian, Pennsylvania State University–York Campus
Anthony Kellman, Augusta College
Bridget Kilgore-Prugh, Pennsylvania State University–York Campus
Marjory Kinney, Bowling Green State University
Catharine B. Kloss, University of Pittsburgh at Johnstown
Joe Kuhl, Augusta College
Andrew J. Kunka, Purdue University
Rosemary Lague, Sacred Heart University
Paula Lambert-Neidigh, Bowling Green State University
Dean Leonard, Clark State Community College
Barbara L'Eplattenier, Purdue University
Karen Madigan, Western Wyoming Community College
Kirsten Marie, Arizona State University
Becky Marquis Ross, Westmoreland County Community College
Marsha Maurer, Augusta College
Oswald Mayers, College of Saint Benedict
Sian Mile, Augusta College
Wendy Miles, Bowling Green State University
Michael Miller, Longview Community College
Jennifer Miroglotta, John Carroll University
John Mumma, Metropolitan Community College
Michele Murton, Westmoreland County Community College
Karen Oberg, Kansas City Kansas Community College
Joan O'Leary, Northern Kentucky University
Donna Padgett, Macon College
Carole Papper, University of Houston-Downtown

Acknowledgments

Les Pollard, Augusta College
Norm Prinsky, Augusta College
Duane Roen, Arizona State University
Marsha Rutter, Southwestern College
Donna Sabella Monheit, Ursinus College
Vicky Sarkisian, Marist College
Jean Schachtschneider, North Hennepin Community College
Don Sevener, Lincolnland Community College
Nancy Shankle, Abilene Christian University
Cheryl Smith, Bowling Green State University
Jim Smith, Augusta College
Lee Smith, University of Houston
Becky Stamm, Columbus State Community College
Marija Stankus-Saulaitis, Northwestern Connecticut Community
    Technical College
Dick Stracke, Augusta College
Nancy Sutherland, Augusta College
Joanna Tardoni, Western Wyoming Community College
Terri Walker, Augusta College
Pat Warren, Cedarville College
Rosemary Winslow, Catholic University of America
Peggy Yonce, Augusta College

Submitting Papers for Publication

To Students and Instructors

We hope that this collection of essays is the third of many editions, and that we'll be able to include more essays from more colleges and universities in the next edition. Please let us see essays you'd like us to consider that were written using *The St. Martin's Guide to Writing*. Send them with this Paper Submission Form and the Agreement Form on the back to English Editor, St. Martin's Press, 345 Park Ave South, New York, NY 10010.

Paper Submission Form

Instructor's Name _____

School _____

Address _____

Department _____

Student's Name _____

Course _____

Writing activity the paper represents _____

This writing activity appears in chapter(s) _____
of *The St. Martin's Guide to Writing*

Agreement Form

I hereby transfer to St. Martin's Press all rights to my essay,

_____

(tentative title), subject to final editing by the publisher. These rights include copyright and all other rights of publication and reproduction. I guarantee that this essay is wholly my original work, and that I have not granted rights to it to anyone else.

St. Martin's Press representative: _____

Student's signature X: _____

Please type

Name: _____

Address: _____

_____

_____

Phone: _____

Please indicate the reader or publication source you assumed for your essay: _____

Write a few sentences about the purpose or purposes of your essay. What did you hope to achieve with your reader?

_____

_____

_____

_____